# LOCAL CIVIL SOCIETY

# Civil Society and Social Change

Series Editors: **Ian Rees Jones** and **Paul Chaney**,
Cardiff University, **Mike Woods**,
Aberystwyth University

---

This series provides interdisciplinary and comparative perspectives on the rapidly changing nature of civil society at local, regional, national and global scales.

## Also in the series:

*City Regions and Devolution in the UK*
By **David Beel, Martin Jones** and **Ian Rees Jones**

*Civil Society and the Family*
By **Esther Muddiman, Sally Power** and **Chris Taylor**

*Civil Society through the Lifecourse*
Edited by **Sally Power**

*The Foundational Economy and Citizenship*
Edited by **Filippo Barbera** and **Ian Rees Jones**

*Putting Civil Society in Its Place*
By **Bob Jessop**

## Forthcoming:

*Analysing the Trust-Transparency Nexus*
By **Ian Stafford, Alistair Cole** and **Dominic Heinz**

Find out more at
**policy.bristoluniversitypress.co.uk/civil-society-and-social-change**

# LOCAL CIVIL SOCIETY
Place, Time and Boundaries

Robin Mann, David Dallimore, Howard Davis,
Graham Day and Marta Eichsteller

First published in Great Britain in 2024 by

Policy Press, an imprint of
Bristol University Press
University of Bristol
1-9 Old Park Hill
Bristol
BS2 8BB
UK
t: +44 (0)117 374 6645
e: bup-info@bristol.ac.uk

Details of international sales and distribution partners are available at
policy.bristoluniversitypress.co.uk

© Bristol University Press 2024

The digital PDF and ePub versions of this title are available Open Access and distributed under the terms of the Creative Commons Attribution-NonCommercial 4.0 International licence ( https://creativecommons.org/licenses/by-nc/4.0/ ) which permits adaptation, alteration, reproduction and distribution for non-commercial use without further permission provided the original work is attributed.

British Library Cataloguing in Publication Data
A catalogue record for this book is available from the British Library

ISBN 978-1-4473-5648-6 hardcover
ISBN 978-1-4473-5649-3 paperback
ISBN 978-1-4473-5650-9 OA ePub
ISBN 978-1-4473-5651-6 OA ePdf

The right of Robin Mann, David Dallimore. Howard Davis, Graham Day and Marta Eichsteller to be identified as authors of this work has been asserted by them in accordance with the Copyright, Designs and Patents Act 1988.

All rights reserved: no part of this publication may be reproduced, stored in a retrieval system, or transmitted in any form or by any means, electronic, mechanical, photocopying, recording, or otherwise without the prior permission of Bristol University Press.

Every reasonable effort has been made to obtain permission to reproduce copyrighted material. If, however, anyone knows of an oversight, please contact the publisher.

The statements and opinions contained within this publication are solely those of the authors and not of the University of Bristol or Bristol University Press. The University of Bristol and Bristol University Press disclaim responsibility for any injury to persons or property resulting material published in this publication.

Bristol University Press and Policy Press work to counter discrimination on
grounds of gender, race, disability, age and sexuality.

Cover design: Hayes Design
Front cover image: Black and white geometric pattern © Freepik.com

# Contents

List of figures vi
Notes on the authors vii
Acknowledgements viii

Introduction 1

1 Civil society as a field of local action 8
2 Community and local civil society: time, continuity and change 24
3 Uncovering local civil society in two Welsh villages 44
4 Civil society through the narratives of place and time 71
5 Civil society and local associational life 86
6 The entwining of civil society, economy and state at local levels 103

Conclusion 125

Notes 128
References 129
Index 143

# List of figures

| | | |
|---|---|---|
| 3.1 | Location map showing our two study sites with the large town of Wrexham and Glyn Ceiriog, the site of Frankenberg's study (1957) | 51 |
| 3.2 | Age by single year (combined) | 57 |
| 3.3 | Marital and civil partnership status | 57 |
| 3.4 | Residents' occupations | 58 |
| 3.5 | Wales Index of Multiple Deprivation (deciles), 2019 | 59 |
| 3.6 | Language spoken | 60 |
| 3.7 | Notions of place identity (average scores from Likert scale, where 6 is 'feel very strongly' and 1 is 'not at all') | 61 |
| 3.8 | What would you say are the best things about living in Rhos/Overton (allowing multiple responses from each respondent)? | 62 |
| 3.9 | What would you say are the worst things about living in Rhos/Overton (allowing multiple responses from each respondent)? | 62 |
| 3.10 | Would you say that over the time you have lived in this area it has got better or worse to live in, or would you say things haven't changed much? | 64 |
| 3.11 | Thinking back to when you were growing up, did you participate in any of the following activities? | 66 |
| 3.12 | Thinking about now, do you participate in any of the following outside the home? | 68 |
| 3.13 | Residents participating by gender | 69 |

# Notes on the authors

**David Dallimore** is an independent researcher and Honorary Research Associate at Bangor University. His research interests include third sector policy, volunteering and novel community development approaches.

**Howard Davis** is Professor Emeritus of Social Theory and Institutions at Bangor University, where he was Head of the School of Social Sciences from 1999 to 2007. From 2008 to 2018 he was Co-Director of the Wales Institute of Social and Economic Research and Data (WISERD). His main areas of research are social theories of culture and creativity; cultural formations and transitions in post-Soviet societies; and social identities at local, national and international levels.

**Graham Day** is Emeritus Reader in Sociology at Bangor University and a WISERD Fellow. He has worked extensively on the sociology of Wales, rural sociology, and studies of community and community development. His publications include *Making Sense of Wales* (University of Wales Press 2002) and *Community and Everyday Life* (Routledge 2006). With Robert Miller he edited *The Evolution of European Identities: Biographical Approaches* (Palgrave Macmillan 2013).

**Marta Eichsteller** is Assistant Professor and Ad Astra Fellow in Sociology at University College Dublin. Marta's main areas of research are identity and belonging, migrations, inequalities and the discourses of social justice. Marta is using biographical narrative research in a variety of research designs. She is the author of 'There is more than one way: a study of mixed analytical methods in biographical narrative research' (*Contemporary Social Science* 2019) and 'Migration as a capability: discussing Sen's capability approach in the context of international migration' (*Social Inclusion* 2021).

**Robin Mann** is Senior Lecturer in Sociology at Bangor University and is Co-Director of the Wales Institute of Social and Economic Research and Data (WISERD). His main areas of research are nationalism, civil society, community and migration, and his current research lies with the WISERD Civil Society Research Centre. He is the author (with Steve Fenton) of *Nation, Class and Resentment: The Politics of National Identity in England, Scotland and Wales* (Palgrave Macmillan 2017).

# Acknowledgements

The research for this book was funded by the Economic and Social Research Council (ESRC) (Grant numbers: ES/L009099/1 and ES/S012435/1). The research was one of many projects linked to the Wales Institute of Social and Economic Research and Data (WISERD) Civil Society Research Centre and we are very grateful for this support. We are especially grateful to Dr Sara Louise Wheeler who was an original member of the research team for her work on the project. Above all, however, we would like to thank the people of Rhosllanerchrugog and Overton who generously gave their time, thoughts and memories during the extended interviews which are at the heart of this book.

# Introduction

Civil society is a term which seeks to capture that aspect of life in society where people meet outside the formal political arena to work together as individuals and groups to express their values and further their common interests. The motivation behind this book, and the research reported here, is a recognition that despite renewed interest and enthusiasm for the idea of civil society in general, the operation of civil society at local levels is not well understood. Theories of civil society are often unhelpful in providing a framework for the conduct of field research into its local constitution. In fact, many of the predominant definitions of civil society seem to omit the local altogether or come to view thickly rooted local attachments as antithetical to the generation of progressive civil competencies. Instead, civil society signifies primarily extraverted forms of action and interaction, which contribute to the capacity to act nationally and transnationally in order to challenge forms of economic and state power. But this leaves out of the picture forms of action and association of principally local reach, where membership is defined in more sociable, rather than political, terms. This is the stuff of local community, and there is, therefore, a critical debate to be had around how the terms of civil society, locality and community inter-relate. For this reason, we are drawn to the anthropological definition (for example, see Hann and Dunn 1996) in which civil society refers to a wider range of practices between state and private life, including informal social relations. This approach offers a more open definition, one which is adaptable to local conditions. The aim of this definition, as Hann (1996: 14) states, is 'to shift the debates about civil society away from formal structures and organisations and towards an investigation of beliefs, values and everyday practices'.

At first glance, the proposition that civil society definitions exclude the local might seem odd. After all, so much of what we understand by civil society takes place locally, whether it be participating in clubs and societies in the evenings and at weekends, volunteering, or taking part in community action. Arguably even the most globalised and transnational aspects of civil society are grounded or rooted in specifically localised sites of grassroots action. So whereas much of the focus of the academic literature on civil society is on voluntary organisations and activism in large-scale social movements and protests, for a good number of people their involvement in civil society is structured around the places in which they live, work and frequent.

Data on patterns of volunteering and different forms of participation would appear to support this (Dallimore et al 2018). Most people's everyday participation is in locally orientated groups and societies to do with leisure, sports and other social activities, or focused on neighbourhood and neighbourly concerns. Alongside this, governmental approaches, such as the United Kingdom 2010–15 coalition government's idea of the Big Society, rest on a premise of bringing about an increase in levels of local participation, an approach which was piloted in selected local areas in England. There is also telling evidence that following the advent of COVID-19, 2020 has seen a remarkable growth in spontaneous local cooperation and action (Georgiou 2020), and furthermore that 'this upswing in social solidarity is almost wholly place-based' (Hambleton 2020: 11). However understood, civil society clearly has a local point of reference.

Nevertheless, the local does have a surprisingly uncertain status within civil society theory specifically. While much of the understanding of civil society would include the sorts of local practices referred to earlier, there are other approaches which leave the status of local social relations far less clear. One evident example of this is the way in which local boundaries which distinguish between insiders and outsiders might run counter to a model of civil society in which locals and strangers are seen as deserving equal footing.

This is not a book about the *theory* of civil society per se. Neither is it our intention to provide a rehearsal of the many and various theoretical disagreements. But given that our empirical attention is on local civil society, then it is worth considering some of the ways in which the connection between the idea of civil society and what we understand as the local is less than straightforward. A key reason for this we would argue is to do with the issue of *civility*. Within third sector and volunteering research, there has undoubtedly been a growing recognition of and research endeavour around what McCabe and Phillimore (2009: 7) describe as 'below the radar' activity. This research addresses an important gap in voluntary sector studies which have been over-reliant on broad-brush and quantitative assessments. Conclusions drawn from survey data on change, and possible decline, in participation and social capital can be misleading in so far as they overlook the more informal, less measurable, types of associational life and mutual aid that take place locally. Local qualitative studies suggest this remains vibrant. However, there is also a more fundamental issue, which is to rethink civil society as not *only* an associational and organisational space. Much of what we would class as 'local' civil society does not sit easily within the customary language of volunteering and the third sector. Comprehending the local level requires us to move away somewhat from this particular language of civil society, and to consider the question of civility, in its everyday forms, much more centrally.

The relationship between civil society and civility is a complex one. Civility has no more essential relationship to the 'third' space of associations which dominates our view of civil society than it has, say, to the actions of politicians, governments, employers or markets. By including it as a concern here we not only get to ask critical questions about associational life, but also can approach civil society in a way which is more fitting to the sorts of empirical questions which arise in the conduct of local research. This is not to do away, as some might propose, with the 'sectoral' model of civil society – which locates it as a space between the individual, economy and state – and replace it with one based on civility, but to argue for research models which can grasp its centrality within informal local social life.

In this book, we report on fieldwork carried out in two North Wales villages. This draws us into dialogue with the tradition of social research around community studies and a much larger body of research carried out in local geographical settings. As we will explain, we approach local civil society as constituted by three substantive, interrelated forms of sociality: association, solidarity and civility. While associations and other forms of collective action have been the focus of many previous and recent local studies, it can be argued that it is civility which acts as the continuous thread of these studies over time and across different places. That is, the concern with the inclusion/exclusion of outsiders, the recognition of differences, and the conflicts which emerge as people work together to address common interests and concerns or seek to persuade others to join in shared enterprises. As Hambleton (2020: 57) underlines, 'reciprocity, cooperation, association, connection, solidarity, community – the building blocks of civil society – are largely place-based and local'.

While community and community studies continue to be viewed with varying degrees of scepticism among anthropologists, geographers and sociologists, the practice of carrying out place-based research in specific localities continues. The current growth of interest in conviviality, belonging and sociality continues this resonance with civility in which local associations and spaces emerge as contexts for the recognition and coming together of diverse others. Much of the developing research on conviviality has been conducted in multi-ethnic urban settings. Carrying out research in our small locality settings, we hope to indicate a more complex and nuanced relationship with local attachment and people's temporal relationships to place and community.

Observing different kinds of geographical settings, one forms an impression of the considerable *time* taken to achieve common goals. The picture from our own research sites is that civil society is locally constituted through people's *enduring* and often *lifelong* connections to place. Thus, we need to account for the possibility of rooted, historicised, forms of local identity as productive of civil society themes. In part, this is a question of who or what actors are we talking about. Participation in civil society is a continuum which speaks to variable degrees of commitment of time and labour: at the sharp end, there exists a small number of key individuals whose work in setting up and maintaining local associations, and working with others in the process, has been a long-term commitment, frequently spanning several years. It is questionable whether such commitments are sustainable without strong attachments to the initiative in question, and the place in which it is located. Moreover, some associational and community activities are more time-intensive than others. Some of the local community groups we describe in this book have been running for half a century and more, and have managed in that time to evolve and adapt. In these cases, civility speaks to a recognition and respect of the commitments these individuals make, even where they might come with a pre-emptive sense of ownership or entitlement. Here, the doing of community is indeed a 'continuous act' (Neal et al 2019: 82), and local associations provide a key context for this doing (Neal et al 2019). In building on such insights, it is important to note both temporal variations in the work of actors towards this doing, and also how the work of building community is not just done in 'the here and now' but involves an ongoing engagement with the past and future. Ignoring this runs the risk of ahistoricism.

## Sites, methods and data

The research reported here forms part of a much larger programme of work on civil society undertaken by WISERD (Wales Institute of Social and Economic Research and Data) and funded by the UK ESRC (WISERD Civil Society, Grant Number: ES/L009099/1).

We draw on fieldwork carried out in two contrasting, yet geographically close village sites in the UK, in North East Wales. The first is the large village of Rhosllanerchrugog (popularly known as 'Rhos') with a population of over 9,000, situated some six miles from Wrexham, the largest town in North Wales. The fortunes of the village are closely linked to the rise and subsequent decline of heavy industries in the area during the 19th and 20th centuries. Two local coal mines were a major source of employment for people living in Rhos from the second half of the 19th century. By 1986 both had been closed. There was some employment growth in other industries in the surrounding area, but today little of this remains in Rhos itself. The village has a strong 'post-industrial' feel. It is quite renowned for its record of civic participation, especially in the areas of religion, culture, music and sport.

Our second site, just seven miles away, is the smaller village of Overton, with a population of 3,500. It is a rural village with a long history (the parish church dates from the 14th century) and a mixed population of locals and incomers, many of whom commute to work elsewhere. We selected it because it has a reputation for unusually high levels of voluntary activity and participation. Overton provides many contrasts to Rhos, with factors such as cultural heritage, social class, demography and migration patterns emerging as being important in shaping associative activity. There is also a stark contrast in how the two places relate to Wales and Welsh identity, despite the short distance between them. Rhos has a strong historical connection to Welsh nonconformism and religious revival. There continues to be a high percentage of residents who speak the Welsh language and there are also specific sites, such as the Miner's Institute ('Stiwt') which make frequent appearances in Welsh language culture and media. On the other hand, Overton is characterised far more by cross-border connections with neighbouring English counties and looks to the English towns of Chester and Shrewsbury as much as it does to Wrexham. But there is also the sense in which the people of Overton, and the work of its community council, have had to engage to a greater extent than before with all Wales public bodies, as a consequence of the devolution taking place following the 1998 Government of Wales Act.

The contrasting comparative design in nearby locations ensures that there is a shared context – for example, access to labour markets, infrastructure, and local government structures and funding, yet the villages are quite distinct in other ways. Seeking contrasts as well as similarities allows us to develop a richer understanding of the phenomenon of participation than is gained typically from large-scale surveys, for example.

The fieldwork itself began by mapping the various sites of participation in the two villages through both site visits and collating administrative, historical and public databases for additional contextual information. Preliminary interviews with two managers of local volunteer centres were also carried out as part of our scoping phase. Then, with an emerging picture of the different spaces in which groups and associations meet we were able to identify individual local actors from a cross-section of these groups. Biographical narrative interviews were then carried out with 20 actors within local community groups across the two sites. Where possible we sought to interview volunteers involved in similar types of association across the two localities. Interviewees were selected according to their leading role within local groups. We employed the biographical narrative method (Rosenthal 2004) to get some purchase on changes in civic participation within each locality, in the wider context of family, employment relations and culture. Our emphasis on personal biographies of involvement, therefore, was consistent with a broader actor- and action-oriented approach to civil society, as a means for exploring the interrelated themes of association, civility and solidarity within specific contexts.

Biographical analysis shows time, and action in civil society over time, to be a central component in the work of these individuals. They are not simply participants who make scheduled time commitments, they also do work which promotes and enables the participation of others. Their accounts indicate longstanding commitments to civil life. In some cases this corresponds to their 'community time' within place; in other cases it builds on the accumulating forms of capital built up elsewhere, drawing on capacities and experiences derived from other places. We also gain an appreciation of how the time commitments of actors engaged in community organising interact with, and are potentially disrupted by, the timescales set around funding and other forms of support by local and national government. It is impossible to describe the stuff of local civil society today without thinking about its relationship to the state.

The 20 extended biographical accounts which were at the core of the project were then extended through the wider collection of interview- and field-based data with residents and other actors in different participatory spaces. A 'street survey' of semi-structured interviews was administered with 182 residents (101 in Rhos, 81 in Overton). These were collected in different public places including libraries, along the main streets and at different local events. Informal conversations were also held with people in a variety of public settings such as cafes and shops. We also attended and collected field notes at various events and meetings. We gathered a range of documentary material including historical archives and contemporary records and reviewed internet and social media material related to the two localities. At the conclusion of fieldwork two public engagement events were carried out – one at the Miner's Institute in Rhos and one at the village hall in Overton – providing the opportunity to present our findings and gain feedback from local participants.

Finally, we would argue that this approach, while place-based, also allows for the exploration of boundaries and the different connections and mobilities which work across them. At the individual level, as mentioned, we find local actors whose biographies are not confined to the two places themselves. Groups and associations, while 'housed' in either Rhos or Overton, will draw participants from other places within the wider locale. Some Rhos and Overton residents will also participate or volunteer in the larger centres of Wrexham or Chester. By looking over time, as well as in place, we can also note how some associations re-locate, for example from Rhos to Wrexham, in order to increase membership access and numbers. These flows, albeit within a broader locale, can be traced by getting actors to talk about their knowledge and experience of participation locally. Some boundaries reflect 'internal' distinctions between new and old parts of the villages and sometimes also between Welsh and English people. The people we interviewed and encountered were predominantly, although not exclusively, 'White British' and neither place has experienced anything in the way of large-scale international migration. At the same time, by taking a historical and temporal view, we can also acknowledge how local civil society in both places has always involved movement, mobility and connection, whether this be the European volunteers who helped build the Ponciau Banks Park in the 1930s or the existence of Overton's 'cocoa rooms' in the building where the village hall and library are located today. The use of biographical methods, coupled with some historical data and the broader emphasis on time, has helped us to draw out these spatial and temporal connections.

## Organisation of the book

Following this Introduction, Chapters 1 and 2 provide the theoretical foundations for the book. Chapter 1 reviews definitions of civil society and sets out an approach to civil society as a field of local social action. Chapter 2 discusses the substantive approach to local civil society and links this to debates over community research. It argues for an analysis of local civil society which accounts for time as well as place. Chapters 3 to 6 provide four empirical chapters: Chapter 3 begins with the places themselves and offers a thick comparison of breadth and depth of civil society in two villages, and their location. Evidence is drawn from historical sources (literature, photographs and other documentary evidence), from administrative and demographic data (including maps, census data), observations and from resident narratives. Chapter 4 offers a deep dive into individual biographies. It outlines the importance of long-term emotional links between the individual biography and place, providing insight into power structures and points of access that directly, but informally, underpin the hierarchies of local actors and the opportunities for civil society participation. Chapter 5 looks across to how participation in local settings is made visible through the activities of associations which identify with place, which depend largely on local social ties, and operate mainly within the limits of local space and its boundaries. Finally, Chapter 6 broadens the analysis to consider connections and boundaries between civil society, economy and the state, and the ways these interplay at the local level. The chapter highlights the importance of seeing state and civil society as existing in a relationship characterised by both dialogue and resistance to varying degrees, rather than as separate bounded entities.

# 1

# Civil society as a field of local action

The aim of this chapter is to explain how we are using the concept of civil society in this book and how this informs our approach to researching civil society in two local settings. This entails setting out a sociological approach to the concept, one which is amenable to the qualitative and ethnographic investigations undertaken in the study. In what follows, we provide a discussion of the meaning of civil society and the importance of the 'local' in its formation and dynamics. By the end of the chapter, the case will have been made for studying civil society as a local, action-orientated, phenomenon, and understanding it as a dynamic interaction process which unfolds over time.

## Defining civil society

Civil society is a complex concept, as witnessed by competing definitions, changing historical scope and disputes about its analytical value. It has both descriptive and normative connotations in equal measure. As we explain further on, civil society has been deployed to describe certain types of action and a kind of social space, as well as an 'ideal' towards which we can progress and which provides an evaluative standard against which forms of social life can be judged. This positions civil society close to the idea of 'community' which also has this moral dimension through its association with ideas of 'communion' and solidarity. Inevitably, this leads to debate and disagreement around what constitutes the 'good' or 'civil' society – making civil society an essentially contested concept.

The starting point for many definitions of civil society is to say that it refers to a space which lies between individuals, families and the state. In this sense, civil society constitutes a major building block of any society, positioned between the private sphere and government. Populating this space are various kinds of organisations and institutions: churches, political parties, social movements, voluntary associations, clubs and societies. The precise content and form of the space will vary from context to context, and may expand and contract over time. A sociological approach to civil society – one which can be operationalised for ethnographic investigation – would be to focus on the actors and groups upon which this space rests. This 'action-orientated' approach is key to the definition offered by Kaldor (2003) who refers to civil society as 'the process through which individuals negotiate, argue, struggle against or agree with each other and with the centres of political and economic authority' (2003: 585).

This approach also relates to other perspectives on civil society in which it is defined as a 'field of action' (Falk 1998: 163; Uhlin 2006: 3; Rucht 2011): individuals as members of society develop their social relations, come together to defend and advance their interests, pursue common goals and may also *enjoy* the sociability which comes with this. And if civil society depends on certain critical actors and groups, we need to know about them, their influences and experiences, and the processes through which they get involved. The emphasis on *process* also invites us to consider civil society as taking place *over time*. Thus one important approach would be to pay special attention to the biographies and lived experiences of key individuals who play a critical role in sustaining civil society activity over time, demonstrating their often 'lifelong' commitments to the places and spaces in which they operate, and which have meaning to them.

Following Kaldor, therefore, we advance a 'process-orientated' approach which sees civil society as forming through the actions of certain individuals and groups as they unfold over time within particular socio-spatial settings. However, whereas Kaldor is concerned with the construction of a *global* civil society, we argue for the need to consider how action takes place across different scales, including at the local level, which should not be seen as any less significant. Indeed, as we will argue, there is no intrinsic association between civil society and a particular scale or geography, rural or urban. In taking this position, we would challenge the assumptions of some theorising of a globalising civil society according to which local attachments and commitments are rendered less relevant to the constructing of civil society. Rather we suggest a dynamic view of civil society over time, involving an interplay between institutionalisation, professionalisation and engagements with the local. The tendency to discard the local level can also be related to the emphasis within civil society theory on large-scale collective action, in the sense that the latter needs to be national or transnational in scope. Civil society actors themselves are often defined in collective terms: as classes, social movements, non-governmental organisations. The question of process becomes one of how individuals come together to form larger-scale movements which provide the capacity to challenge centres of economic and political power. But what gets left out of this picture are all those local associational aspects of social life which are not necessarily to be characterised as engaged in acts of resistance, or motivated by ambitions for large-scale social change, but which are sites of civility and sociability. By contrast, Robert Putnam's work on social capital (Putnam 2000) puts involvement in local associations at the centre, but only in terms of their contribution to maintaining democracy and citizenship at the societal level. Hence his approach to civil society has been questioned for ignoring the uncivil and undemocratic elements of associational life (Berman 1997).

Although we are placing actors themselves at the centre, we should also acknowledge that actors and groups, while essential, are not themselves enough. The actors and groups which constitute civil society should not be seen as wholly separate from the economic and political structures surrounding them. These structures are intrinsically connected to civil society either by facilitating or constraining the field of action. These connections are also essential for advocating civil society as a space for solidarity and dialogue, while at the same time maintaining a critical stance towards governmental championing of this very space. This is no more evident than with the UK Conservative-Liberal Democrat coalition government's 2010–15 flagship Big Society initiative, which while appearing to invest in and promote certain kinds of local civic action took place within a broad period which saw the undermining of the material and political conditions in which individuals and groups achieve common goals (Levitas 2012). The need to pay attention to such connections also resonates with feminist critiques of the distinction between civil society and the domestic sphere (Pateman 1988) which have continuing significance in the context of austerity around the way voluntary activities tend to rely heavily on unpaid, predominantly female, work. Thus, we also need to pay attention to the material conditions on which the actions of individuals rest.

In the next section, we provide a more in-depth conceptual overview to explain how we come to adopt this position. There are contrasting ways of defining civil society, not all of which are consistent with the approach outlined earlier. The inherent multiplicity of the concept has to do partly with how it has emerged from contrasting modes of social and political thought. It is therefore worth understanding in more detail how civil society has been defined over time, and how the space it defines can be seen to be changing.

## Emergence and development of the concept

The first real effort to define civil society sociologically is often traced to key scholars of the early modern period, Hobbes, Locke and Ferguson (Seligman 1992; Wagner 2006). For these scholars there is no evident separation between state and civil society. Rather civil society is a type of state characterised by the social contract – a 'society governed by agreed laws for the purposes of peace and productivity' (Kaldor 2003: 584). A special place is granted to the Scottish enlightenment thinker, Adam Ferguson (1723–1816) who in his *Essay on the History of Civil Society* (1767) defined the concept as a space of moral sentiments – the 'sense of a shared public' in which the pursuit of private interests could be reconciled with a commitment to the common good (Seligman 1992: 5).

By the end of the 19th century, the enlightenment understanding of civil society had fallen out of favour (Keane 2009: 461). With growing division of labour, industrialisation and population growth, the enlightenment vision of an autonomous civil society regulated by normative consensus gave way to the emerging sociology of modern society which emphasised social differentiation and class struggles, and in which social integration depended on some measure of bureaucracy or state planning (Alexander 1998: 5; Pérez-Díaz 2014: 816–7). Efforts to reconstruct the concept within late 20th-century social and political theory also acknowledge the central contributions of Hegel, Tocqueville and Gramsci as thinkers who carried the idea of civil society over to the 19th and 20th centuries (Alexander 1998: 3–8). Furthermore, the idea of civil society displays a strong affinity with themes of community, and its alleged demise through modernity and modernisation, within the work of early sociologists, especially Tönnies ([1887] 2001) and Durkheim (1893).

In Chapter 3, we will explain our empirical focus on the 'village' for the exploring of local civil society. It is worth briefly discussing at this point, therefore, how enlightenment and early sociological conceptualisations provide some indications as to their spatial reference points. In *De Cive* (1651) Hobbes explicitly equates civil society with life in the 'city'. While this association between civil society and the city or urban has not been consistently applied, it nevertheless indicates the way ideas of civil society have been grounded in rural-urban distinctions, albeit often over-drawn. Twentieth-century writings on rural-urban comparisons routinely associate the city with large, fragmented and individualised populations, in need of relationships of civility or civilisation, whereas the rural has been viewed as prone to established popular and parochial ways of thinking (Savage and Warde 1993). For this reason it might be tempting to draw a sharp distinction between civil society and the 'local community', whereby the latter refers to collective actions and identities arising from place-based ties, whereas the former is civic- and market-orientated, setting it apart from narrowly local social relations. This is evident in Tönnies' ([1887] 2001) famous distinction between *Gemeinschaft* (often translated as 'community') and *Gesellschaft* (translated sometimes as 'society' and also as 'association'). More recently, this sociological classic has been re-issued under the title *Community and Civil Society* (Tönnies [1887] 2001), which begs precisely this question.

In his analysis of the enlightenment concept of civil society, Seligman (1992: 68–9) makes clear the parallels with the views of Adam Ferguson, who believed that it is through:

> 'freeing' of the individual from the traditional, primordial and particular solidarities based on kinship and territorial identities that we identify with the forms of modern society ... these ties were defined no

longer by a tradition of primordial 'givenness' (membership in a territorial collective) but by ... shared (moral) commitments. (Seligman 1992: 68–9)

Accordingly, it is the break-up of local and pregiven identities – the transition from community to association – that make civil society a possibility (Seligman 2000: 15). That is, civil society corresponds to an imagined political community rather than the substantive local community. However, and also in contrast to civil society's associations with the city and the urban, Somers' (1993) historical research on 18th-century England has shown how the roots of democratic movements laid with village cultures and rural industrial working-class people.

We will return to these issues in more detail. To sum up for the time being, between the early modern period and the late 20th century the defining of civil society can be characterised by an increasingly narrow specification as a more developed sociology emerged: *civil society as state* (social contract); *civil society as the space between individual, family and state* (Hegel, Marx) and then on to *civil society as the space in opposition to these structures and to those of the economy and market* (Gramsci). The concept is narrowed even further by Alexander (2006) who positions civil society, or in his preferred language, the 'civil sphere', as one sphere among several other 'non-civil' spheres, including, importantly for us, the sphere of 'geographically bounded regional communities' (Alexander 2006: 404). The implication of this is that regional and local community identities have the potential both to undermine, as well as facilitate, the building of solidarity within civil society.

## Late 20th- and early 21st-century reformulations

After a period of relative eclipse, during which other terms, such as citizenship, community and the public sphere, seemed to usurp its place, the idea of civil society re-emerged during the 1980s with the collapse of communism in the former Soviet Union and Eastern Europe, as well as with the democratisation taking place in other countries around the same time, especially in Latin America (Alexander 1998; Keane 1988). In these contexts, civil society came to be viewed as a vital reference point for capturing the collective actions, interests and voices of large swathes of national citizens in expressing their opposition to colonial empires and totalitarian state regimes, as well as the infrastructure of independent civil/civic relations and groupings needed to support this. This was unlike the classic definitions described earlier which saw civil society as territorially bounded, and closely affiliated with the state. Hegel, for example, saw a territorially strong and militarily secure state as necessary for civil society to flourish (Kaldor 2003: 585–6). In contrast, the revived concept in Latin America and Eastern Europe was anti-state in its opposition to despotic regiments. Far from providing the vital organising framework, 'Big State' was now the problem and civil society was counterposed to the state as a realm of 'freedom' and spontaneity. However, in a pioneering collection of anthropological studies of Eastern and Central Europe, Hann and Dunn (1996) make a valuable contribution to the civil society debate. Reflecting on the intellectual celebration of civil society in relation to the removal of Soviet rule, they question the notion that civil society was making a sudden unexpected appearance, and that people were previously unable to form associations independent of an all-consuming communist state. In an earlier paper Hann (1992) stresses that there is 'another level of cooperation based upon informal networks deeply embedded in the local community' which 'must be taken into account' (Hann 1992: 161).

In the 1990s, political and policy interest in civil society in the West was extended in at least three important ways: as a debate over the decline of civic participation in Western societies and its consequences for social capital (Putnam 2000; Walzer 1992); as part of neo-liberal justifications for the rolling back of state responsibilities and enlarging the role of the third and private (market) sectors in taking over some aspects of service delivery; and finally in promotion of the role of non-governmental organisations (NGOs) within international development policy (Lewis 2002; Pearce 2002).

In the latter case, the increase in the number of international NGOs during the 1990s was seen as a precursor to an emerging global civil society based around the power of international institutions vis-à-vis nation-states (Taylor 2004). Big institutions themselves, such as the World Bank and the International Monetary Fund, took up the cause of civil society (Dawson and Bhatt 2001). Paradoxically, by the beginning of the 21st century the anti-globalisation protests against the actions of these very institutions would come to define much of the idea of a 'globalising' civil society. To this we can also add some indications of an emerging globalising public sphere, both as a consequence of advances in global communication technologies and in recognition of issues which are inherently global in nature including climate change, environment, demography and poverty (Castells 2008).

A powerful current of recent thought takes us towards the action-oriented field of social movements and citizenship. In their analysis of the historical development of civil society, Cohen and Arato (1992: 492) emphasise the dynamic interplay between social movements and institutions in civil society. Struggles and campaigns of individuals and groups against the state have led to the institutionalisation of civil rights and the establishing of structures and spaces for civil society activity. As Cohen and Arato explain, while these help to structure the field of action, they also entail compromises with the state and market, and therefore there is a continuous interaction between formal and informal, institutionalised and spontaneous/resistant elements: for example, between campaigns which become absorbed into party and thereby into state, and those which remain as movements, on the outside. Following these broad parameters, we can see civil society characterised as a plural and diverse, action-oriented, field, in which individuals and groups are oriented to the realising of the good society, but also one in which the field itself is characterised by tensions between institutionalisation and autonomy or withdrawal.

Furthermore, there is an acknowledgement that actors and groups in civil society, and their actions, may depend on or derive resources from outside the intermediate space of civil society itself – such as economic, family, or state support. Thus we get the idea of boundary relationships between civil society, state and market which can either be destructive or facilitative (Alexander 2006). This raises particular issues about the interface between civil society and state: the state can work with and assist civil society, but can also capture it. Kaldor (2003: 589) describes NGOs as 'tamed' social movements – institutionalised and professionalised, but which as a consequence lose their local grassroots connections as they become part of the system of global governance. This has a temporal dimension because they reflect movements 'on the wane'. This point about NGOs has led to post-structuralist and Foucauldian analyses which have been concerned with how *representation* obscures the fluidities between civil society and the state (Gøtzsche-Astrup 2019). In other words, organisations which might understand themselves, and be understood by others, as signifying civil society but are actually part of the state. Concern here with the *transactional* also links us to the Gramscian understanding of civil society. According to Crehan (2002: 103), in Gramsci's work we can see that the relationship between state and civil society is one which continually shifts, in order to capture particular manifestations of power. Gramsci not only indicates both the reach of the state [which] can include civil society: '"State" should be understood not only the apparatus of government, but also the private apparatus of "hegemony", or civil society' (SPN 261, cited in Crehan 2002: 103). But also their *entwining*: 'The state and civil society, that is, do not represent two bounded universes, always and forever separate but rather a tangled knot of power relations which, depending on the questions we are interested in, can be disentangled into different assemblages or threads' (Crehan 2002: 103).

While allowing for the autonomy of civil society to some degree, we nevertheless gain from Gramsci a firm steer towards the civil society-state relation as one characterised by continuing mutual influence rather than separateness, and therefore the need to investigate those contexts and spaces which remain 'inaccessible to centralised political power' and creatively 'outstrip its reach' (see Buchowski 1996: 82). Building on these insights, we can discuss how investigations into civil society as a field of action have proceeded in different directions, and at different levels of analysis – national, global and local.

## Civil society, public sphere and the national scale

It is noteworthy how much civil society theorising emphasises the collective framework within which civil society operates and in so doing continues to prioritise a nationally framed public sphere. Certainly, a major division within the civil society literature appears to be whether it is seen as the coming together of a unified collectivity ('peoplehood') or remains a diverse set of organisations and groups. In the first meaning, civil society overlaps with civic and the public, and is synonymous with the growth of a public sphere, distinct from and in opposition to a private, familial, or domestic sphere.

This view of civil society as acting on a scale and level well above the local is reflected in some of the most prominent theoretical efforts to reconstruct the concept around the turn of the 21st century. A key contributor to this theoretical reconstruction, Alexander (1997; 1998; 2006), takes a particular view as to the scale at which civil society takes form. Alexander's overriding concern is to inject a much needed sociological realism to civil society scholarship, in order to counter some of the more idealist and abstract philosophical conceptualisations. He makes two critical points which are especially pertinent for us here. Firstly, he refers explicitly to civil society as a realm of social solidarity, and contends that it is through the territory of the nation state that this solidarity is best realised:

> [Civil society is] the arena in which social solidarity is defined in universalistic terms. It is the we-ness of the national community taken in the strongest possible sense, the feeling of connectedness to 'every member' of that community that transcends particular commitments, narrow loyalties and sectional interests. Only this kind of solidarity can provide a thread of identity uniting people dispersed by religion, class, ethnicity or race. (Alexander 1997: 118)

This comment bears a strong resemblance to Anderson's (1991) vision of the nation as an 'imagined' community. In other words, Alexander likens civil society with nation, as a 'bounded societal community coterminous with the state' (see Cohen 2007: 47). Secondly, Alexander sees civil society as *fixed* to a national territory. Furthermore, in the process he refers interchangeably to place, space and territory. Where he does mention the local, it is in the historical context of a transition from local primordial territories to national civil societies. Similarly Calhoun (2007), while avoiding any essentialist view of their relation, nevertheless sees nationalism as positive for the construction of civil society: 'nationalism encourages identification of individuals not with locality per se, not with the webs of their specific interpersonal relationships, but with an abstract category. This category of nation may be a helpful mediation between the local and the global' (Alexander 2007: 100). For Alexander and others, then, the scale of civil society is quite explicitly to be equated with the territory of the national state. And the degree to which the national states are cognate to civil society relates to how they provide an arena for civil, political and social rights, and for determining access to or exclusion from them.

The key national actors would then appear to be social movements, intellectuals and also the media and public sphere. Social movements bring civil society into being through challenging and superseding the reductive practices of social solidarity, acting to expand the boundaries of social solidarity in ways that are more inclusive. Participation in civil society is linked to the development of an impartial public sphere and this entails setting aside one's local identities and statuses. Movements are thus central to civil society but so are the media and public sphere as the crucial mechanisms through which the performances of powerful movements achieve a wider societal impact and gain public attention. Thus, Calhoun (2011) states that among the defining aspects of a public sphere are forms of media which 'transcend locality' (2011: 11), while Pusey (1998: 145) claims that 'social movements create new norms, identities and solidarities that transcend the spatial and temporal structures of particular communities' (1996: 52). In these definitions we are dealing with civil society organised at a particular scale, the national, which appears to render the local superfluous, irrelevant or, as we will see in many versions, even antithetical to civil society. For example:

> Civil society can be a place where citizens retreat into insular and defensive groups. It can be a place where particularism and difference define participation and where the self-organization of citizens contributes to a general atmosphere of distrust and misunderstanding. It is not the case, as sometimes implied by communitarians, that active associational life is good in and of itself. Associations, clubs, churches, and of course, families, can and do promote antidemocratic illiberal ideas and where they do bad civil society emerges. Bad civil society is one that promotes or is hospitable to particularist civility – that is, civility that does not cross group boundaries. How do we protect ourselves from this risk? (Chambers 2002: 101; see also Meyer and Hyde 2004)

## Global and transnational civil society

More recently, work on civil society has questioned in effect the primacy given to the nation and its territory, by turning towards the crystallisation of a global or transnational civil society. Here civil society is not bounded to nation and state, but is open-ended, and shifts in relation to the ascendancy of global, and sub-national, economic and political actors. Kaldor's account of global civil society begins with the role of 'new social movements' – 'The explosion of movements, groups, networks and organisations that engage in global or transnational debate' (2003: 583). Castells (2008) also stresses the extent to which the public sphere is and has been globalised. While acknowledging that the spread is uneven, globalisation has brought about certain capacities which enable the development of a global civil society, especially with regard to technology and the emergence of 'global networks'. Much of Castells' argument can be seen to rest on an understanding of how civil society is undergoing change – its areas of growth and decline. On one hand, social movements addressing the concerns of marginalised groups are growing, especially organisations mobilising on transnational issues. The action of new social movements sees civil society as increasingly operating across territorial state borders and through the inter-connections across local and global scales. For Castells (2008), the importance of the public sphere is that it constitutes the space in which civil society and state interact. He builds on Habermas' definition of the public sphere ' as networks for communicating information and points of view' (1996: 360). In the public sphere, 'people come together as citizens ... to influence the political institutions of society' (Castells 2008: 78). He then proceeds to say the following about civil society: 'Civil society is the organized expression of these views; and the relationship between the state and civil society is the cornerstone of democracy. Without an effective civil society capable of structuring and channelling citizen debates over diverse ideas and conflicting interests, the state drifts away from its subjects' (2008: 78).

In this passage, there is a high degree of isomorphism between public sphere and civil society – as space and as the content of that space respectively. But not all, by any means, of what makes up civil society can be viewed in this *scaled-up* way – simply and solely as organising diverse interests to challenge the state. Given Castells' own point that 'not everyone, or everything, is globalised', a lot of what makes up actual society is left out of the picture. By itself, this perspective would ignore that large part of the field of action which continues to be quite *local* in scope and orientation – and is characterised more by experiences and practices of everyday local sociability than by taking part in a movement with global pretensions. It is here that we might find for example that array of small-scale sports and leisure clubs, interest groups, informal support systems and local associations which constitute the lifeblood of a vibrant local civil society.

## Local-global interconnectedness: progressive and regressive local civil society

In much recent social movement literature, far from setting the local and global in opposition, the emphasis has been on cross-scalar connections – as recognised by the introduction of terms like 'translocal' and 'glocal'. Scholarship has emphasised how a global civil society is produced through various kinds of located and materialised activity, such as through grassroots organisations and informal groupings which act as latent resources for mobilisation into larger transnational movements. Geographically orientated research into social movements has also highlighted the significance of the local as a mobilising tool, or as providing politicised sites of protest, and nodes in transnational, or translocal, activist networks (Routledge 2003; McFarlane 2009). Places (such as neighbourhoods) function as sites of political activism, as a mobilising resource (Rootes 2008). In these and other ways social movement research pays heed to spatiality: for instance Diani (2005) on the engagements of local civil society organisations with global issues; Sassen (2002) on the microsites of global civil society and McIlwaine (2007) on transnational civil society.

These contributions nevertheless retain a predominant emphasis upon the urban, the city and on movements which have a transnational shape. So, Diani (2005) provides an in-depth empirical analysis of local-global civil society dynamics in the two UK cities of Bristol and Glasgow. Focusing on organisations mobilising around environmental, social exclusion, migrant and minority ethnic issues, many of which are local branches of UK-wide organisations, Diani finds evidence of growing interest in action on global issues through local civil society organisations, pointing also to how global agendas are reshaping the organisations in question. It is the 'density of political and civic cultures in large cities which localises global civil society in people's lives' (Sassen 2002: 218).

If global civil society, as defined by Kaldor (2003), refers to those organisations which have a 'global or international frame of reference' then we have increasing evidence of local civil society meeting this definition. However, as mentioned at the outset of our discussion, the civil society concept has both empirical and normative elements which play into concerns about what might be regarded as progressive and regressive sorts of local social relations. The shift of academic research and debates about civil society to the global and transnational levels has been associated with efforts to associate civil society with cosmopolitanism, in what Calhoun describes as a 'basic rhetorical opposition between the liberal cosmopolitan and the illiberal local' (Calhoun 2003: 532). Thus debates concerning the relationship between cosmopolitanism and the parochial also have relevance for understandings of civil society. The working assumption of the cosmopolitan literature is that local attachments produce 'a politics hooked around the myth of a regionalized identity' (Amin 2004: 37). Very often, cosmopolitan civil society and global consciousness are counterposed to the alleged parochialisms and exclusions of local life. With regard to our own field of research, this has profound consequences because identifying local progressiveness with a cosmopolitan or global sense of place (Massey 1991a) shapes how we might see the distinction between urban and rural places, and the very nature of community.

Tomaney (2013) provides us with a cogent critique of cosmopolitan conceptualisations of civil society in which local identities and outlooks are associated primarily with regressive and populist politics, and therefore regarded as implying an *uncivil* society. He offers a more positive view of the potential for civil society at local level, illustrating how 'parochial' outlooks and other valorisations of the local may provide the starting points for civil society: 'A parochial outlook values the local, its culture and solidarities, as a moral starting point and locus of ecological concern and a site for the development of virtues including commitment, fidelity, civility and nurture' (2013: 659). So, 'local identities may provide the conditions for a "progressive" mode of dwelling' (2013: 662) within the wider processes described by Massey (1991a). We believe that this makes the validity of the cosmopolitan/local and progressive/regressive distinctions a matter for empirical investigation, rather than theoretical assertion.

## Place, rural-urban distinctions and the nature of community

Undoubtedly we can note the close affinity between the proposed duality of localism and cosmopolitanism and conventional accounts of the nature of community, often embedded within rural and urban distinctions. Bell and Newby (1976: 286) record how for a long time 'community' with its implications of harmony, stability, integration and consensus came to be understood among sociologists as a rural phenomenon, whereas the industrial (and later post-industrial) city was defined as non-community, redolent of conflict, disorder, isolation and above all class division. They trace this dichotomy to Tönnies' 'most mischievous legacy', his tendency to ground different types of social relationships (*Gemeinschaft* and *Gesellschaft*) in particular patterns of settlement and geographical locales. Although Tönnies did not intend his concepts to take on a spatial (or scalar) connotation – community versus association representing a choice which was *always and everywhere* present in human sociation – nevertheless his empirical examples were especially prone to place *gemeinschaft* within the traditional rural setting.

From then on there was a lengthy debate about the validity of the urban/rural contrast, associated with an escalating critique of the 'rural'. Classic formulations of urban social life (Simmel 1903; Wirth 1938) imply the continual threat of incivility: city populations are large, anonymous, impersonal, and without adequate regulation there is constant risk of collapse into individualism and the Hobbesian 'war of all against all'. The creation of relations of civil society offers one solution to this problem of scale. Yet we should note how when theories of civil society were first proposed, the vast majority of people lived in what by current standards were extremely small urban concentrations: during Hobbes' lifetime, no English city outside London had more than 35,000 inhabitants. By 1800, when Ferguson wrote his history of civil society, Bristol, then second in size only to London, had reached around 45,000. Today we would regard these as small towns. In this historical context, the urban, and any distinction this has from the rural, is ambiguous. In Hobsbawm (1962: 20–1), for example the urban is 'no less an aspect of the "small", "provincial" towns ... where townsmen looked down upon the surrounding countryside ... almost as closed in, as the village'. Very obviously, scale and its attendant difficulties is a relative matter, and it is not scale per se which introduces the risk of incivility.

Later urban sociologists switch towards a view in which it is the openness and relative privacy of the city which enables the benefits of diversity, cosmopolitanism, freedom and progress; they tend to see the danger in the small, inward-looking, socially homogeneous world of the village and small town. The continuing legacy of the earlier work can be seen in arguments such as that of Young (1986: 248) that the ideal of 'community' is undesirably utopian because it 'devalues and denies difference', failing to see the potential in close and face-to-face relations for alienation and violence. It reveals, she says, a 'desire for unity and wholeness which generates borders, dichotomies and exclusion'. Similarly the geographer David Harvey (1989) attacks the tendency to 'fetishise' place, locality and social groupings by attributing to them stable, coherent and uncontradictory qualities. He contends that emphasis on the local 'enhances certain kinds of sensitivities (but) totally erases others and thereby truncates rather than emancipates the field of political engagement and action' with inevitably reactionary consequences (Harvey 1996: 353). In similar expressions of this binary opposition we are told that 'community is about closed systems and reified relations and city about openness and change. This difference is predicated upon different life-worlds and modes of appropriating space' (McBeath and Webb 1997: 249). Consequently we are warned that 'any movement founded on concern for community life is liable to degenerate into some form of Fascist authoritarianism' (Tam 1998: 32). Policy interventions such as New

Labour's Third Way approach at the beginning of this century are criticised for falling into a 'romance of local community' (Amin 2005) which treats (some, but not all) places as spatially circumscribed, focused on their own problems and concerns, incapable of connecting with or influencing the world outside – altogether too localised. Such warnings about the hazards of community are endlessly circulated until they become taken for granted (Back 2009).

However, others, such as Massey (1991b) point out that these claims are themselves examples of reification and reductionism. Challenging Harvey's belief that a focus on place and the local is by nature anti-progressive, she says there is no necessary reason for such a negative interpretation, since: 'It is people, not places in themselves, that are reactionary or progressive' (1991b: 278). Places are intrinsically dynamic, and capable of carrying multiple meanings, since they are constructions out of the intersections and interactions of concrete social relations and social processes (1991b: 277). Thus Massey argues for a sense of place which is 'extraverted', about movement, linkage and contradiction, and with a multiplicity of potential meanings for different actors. In this she echoes conclusions of an earlier generation of social geographers: Pahl (1966) among others decided that attempting to pin patterns of social relationships or forms of consciousness to specific geographical milieux was 'a singularly fruitless exercise' while Gans (1968) agreed that 'ways of life do not coincide with settlement patterns'. As an example of how urban and rural might cut across each other, Pahl and Gans employed the idea of the 'urban village' – those districts or neighbourhoods within cities which retained many of the characteristics of the rural way of life: bounded, homogeneous, sociable (see also Benson and Jackson 2013). In their analyses, aspects of the rural penetrated into the urban. Elsewhere, in some of the classic rural community studies, influences flowed from the opposite direction: Rees (1950) in his account of rural Wales argued that 'urban' influences were infiltrating (and ultimately destroying) the rural. All these contributions drew on empirical evidence and investigation, yet were riddled with ethical and evaluative judgements about the quality of life and value standards evident in different places.

Bell and Newby (1976) reiterated that there was no logical reason to assume that the desired content of human relationships – identity, affection, integration and so on – could be found only in certain specific forms of territoriality and social systems. The inclination to believe otherwise is to fall into what Purcell calls the 'local trap', the tendency to assume something inherent about the local scale (2006: 1923). As we have seen this can take a negative form, but it also has its positive or idealised equivalent, where for instance: 'the local is assumed to be desirable; it is preferred a priori to larger scales. What is desired varies and can include ecological sustainability, social justice, democracy, better nutrition, and food security' (Born and Purcell

2006: 195). We can neither assume that 'community' is automatically good nor bad – rather it is double-sided and capable of both, having aspects of both 'heaven and hell' (Barrett 2015).

From a standpoint of social criticism and political engagement, Williams (1983: 124) offers a different way of approaching the problem. Rather than thinking in terms of community as 'an abstract aggregate with an arbitrary general interest' similar to the open-ended universalism of civil society as posited by Alexander (1997) and others, he insists on always maintaining a reference to actual people and places. For him, meaningful community involves the kind of strong attachment people develop to 'the place where they live and want to go on living, where generations of ... effort and care have been invested, and which new generations will inherit' (Williams 1983: 124). Drawing on his own experience and biography, he registers the potential for 'a level of social obligation ... conferred by the fact of seeming to live in the same place and in that sense to have a common identity. And from this sense there were acts of kindness beyond calculation, forms of mutual recognition even when they were wild misinterpretations of the world outside' (1983: 113). In these terms, community is less a matter of scale than the quality of relationships among neighbours. At the same time, Williams warned against idealising this possibility, showing in both scholarly and fictional practice (Williams 1960; 1973; 1979) that the actual experience of living in such a community was often fragmented and limited, involving both creative and destructive processes, so 'what is experienced again and again, is not only closeness and sympathy but conflict, loss, frustration and despair' (Williams 1987: 173).

The insight derived from a substantial body of geo-spatial analysis is that geographical scale is a fundamentally relational concept (Agnew 1987; Heley and Jones 2012), and that the idea of scale implies a set of interscalar relationships. The meaning of a 'local' scale, for example, only comes alive in relation to other, larger scales. Moreover, because scales represent larger and larger portions of geographical space, relations among scales are characterised by embeddedness: the local scale is embedded in the regional, then the national scale, which is embedded in the global scale. Each scale is inseparably defined by and tied to the others. However, the particular relationships among scales are outcomes of social production. The hegemony of the national-scale state, to take our earlier example, did not define the national simply as larger than the local, but established the nation as the dominant scale of state sovereignty and the local as a subordinate scale. Thus, decisions made by local-scale state bodies can be overturned by national-scale bodies. Any move towards localisation, conversely, advocates a new relationship between the local scale and larger ones as power becomes devolved to lower level areas (Born and Purcell 2006). It follows that 'local' actors and groups are not wholly bound to their particular local milieu, but capable of acting in ways which make visible the connections across time and space. Detailed local studies show this, pointing to the historical importance of connections to other places, and other scales; only an unduly simplified reading misses this.

## Conclusion

In this opening chapter we have put forward a sociological approach which focuses on civil society as a field of action, and takes an empirical focus on the individuals and groups acting within this field, and the processes through which these actions take form, to consider how such actions produce and reproduce the space within a variety of contexts. We have also shown how many understandings of civil society would view strongly knit local ties as inimical to civil society, and as a barrier to it. But we have argued that this is an outdated and one-sided view, fixated on civil society as a national territorialised entity, which has now been translated from the national to the global domain. Other perspectives point to the intrinsic connections between local ties and broader participation, or to the everyday reciprocities. Some suggest the opening up, stretching and linkages between local, national and transnational civil society. Rather than assuming any intrinsic normative association between civil society and any particular scale – for example, the global as desirable or the local as undesirable – instead we should consider how actions within these fields operate across different scales as part of a historical dynamic of expansion and contraction over time. In this sense, portrayals of local communities as antithetical to civil society can be seen as 'synchronic' representations of place, a kind of 'presentism' which emphasises the 'here' and 'now' but which fails to take time, history and biography into account. For example, local civil society spaces and institutions, which were formed through wider movements and associations, such as trade unions and the labour movement may now be viewed as too local or too parochial, and thereby as having been 'left behind' by the forces of global transformation. In the next chapter we will consider how local place-based studies can be enlivened by tracing these wider civil society connections across time and place.

# 2

# Community and local civil society: time, continuity and change

This chapter proposes the view that local civil society be examined and understood with reference to community and local studies carried out over the long term. To do this it draws on studies carried out in a wide range of geographical settings, leaving our next chapter (Chapter 3) to focus on both Wales and small village settings. In the previous chapter we described how ideas of community and civil society are often thought to occupy the same social space, both lying as they do between the individual, family and the state. They are also ideas which combine, and are often seen to confuse, the empirical state of affairs with the normative ideal yet to be achieved. In the analysis of place and locality, however, there has been a clear shift among sociologists and geographers away from community as a framework for research practice, especially in urban and big-city contexts. Specific charges against community studies include the tendency to produce homogenous accounts of place, and by romanticising local community life, to ignore or underplay exclusion, and indeed, incivility (Cohen 1997). In response, a cosmopolitan re-orienting of place and locality is advocated, based on research imaginations capable of attending to diversity and the interplay between local and global levels (Back 2009). The implication of the cosmopolitan method is not only that a shift away from community, and traditional approaches, is necessary for capturing the progressive elements of local social life, but also that 'bounded' communities are not generative of civil society. Examples of such approaches for linking local and global within place-based studies include Massey's 'progressive sense of place' (1991) and 'throwntogetherness' (2005: 140), and Savage et al's (2005) theory of 'elective belonging'. These provide us with invaluable starting points for building a picture of local civil society. Through their emphasis on volition, choice and freedoms linked to attachments and practices of place, they posit relatively open boundaries which place strangers on an equal if not greater footing to those who are locally 'born and bred'.

These approaches relate to other appreciations of place around conviviality which has lately gained interest as a term describing both the everyday social relations as well as the qualities of places themselves which enable 'different others' and 'strangers' to become acquainted in civil and friendly ways (Gilroy 2004; Wessendorf 2014). These ideas are commonly asserted against their presumed opposites – other kinds of place attachments and relations in settings where multicultural or other forms of diversity have not become commonplace (for example, 'provincial' or White-dominated localities) which have been associated with the regressive, and thereby with the uncivil. This would include forms of identity deemed to rest upon boundary and closure. As Back (2009: 201) notes, cosmopolitan methods have tended to be asserted in opposition to the 'parochialism of community studies'. Such oppositions, however, are difficult to sustain when set against what is itself a very large and diverse body of empirical research. As we will show, it is possible to find a number of continuities and synergies between civil society themes and the sociological tradition of community research. There is also the risk that the task of attending the local and global itself is embarked upon in an ahistorical way which fails to grasp how studies carried out across the 20th century were already beginning to respond to these criticisms.

What this body of empirical local studies would indicate is the need for far greater nuance in how we might ground the idea of civil society in particular kinds of places and times. Places which exhibit regressive forms of identity and consciousness may also display some of the qualities we associate with the idea of civil society. As Back argues, these nuances require close attention and observation of local life which can acknowledge not only 'the mourning of the passing of a golden age' and 'racist melancholy', but also the rituals of sociality and 'homely co-existence' (2009: 209).

What we claim here is that we can provide a more subtle and balanced view of local civil society by situating it more thoroughly in the analysis of time and place, that is, by patterning its historical and spatial continuities and discontinuities. In doing so, we seek to build upon developments within the understanding of 'community' which treat it as a fluid social construct, capable of negotiating and handling similarity and difference, through complex forms of representation and meaning (Day and Murdoch 1993; Day 1998; Liepins 2000; Barrett 2015). These forms and meanings are not static, and cannot be specified independently of context, since they are outcomes of social action within a dynamic field of localised social interaction (Abram 1998). Barrett (2015) expresses this well when he writes:

> The paradox of community is that it can represent both heaven and hell for its members ... Community is a site for colonising practices that shroud difference and marginalise dissenting voices. But to deny that solidarity can exist in a community setting is not much better than trumpeting value consensus. We need a model that can adequately capture both patterns of attachment and exclusion. (2015: 184)

This chapter, then, aims to show the ongoing value of previous community and local studies for understanding local civil society, and their importance as reference points for our pictures of change over time. In reconsidering a broad range of classic and recent local studies, we can uncover the normative continuities between enduring local attachments and the civil society idea. With the use of ethnographic, historical and biographical methods, our empirical chapters will then aim to show how local connections to place, and those extending beyond, can be explored.

## Substantive elements of local civil society in the context of social change

To begin, we must clarify more precisely what might be understood by *local* civil society, how it has undergone change, and the significance that both place and time have for how it takes form. While acknowledging that what we understand by local civil society is multifaceted, and often contested, we can concern ourselves with three broad themes: associations (and their voluntary nature); civility (including everyday acts of acknowledgement and recognition between diverse others and strangers); and solidarity (relating to collective action and mutual aid). Each of these themes can be found in local studies. For example, Jackson's (1968) 1960s study of Huddersfield, an industrial town in the North of England, reported involvement in a range of working-class associations – working men's clubs, brass bands, bowling clubs, trade unions – which formed an important part of class identity and culture. These bodies were often defined in opposition to equivalent middle-class associations, and were also sites of exclusion for women. Stacey (1960) depicts the town of Banbury with a diagram which maps a profusion of local organisations, again clustered along lines of class, gender, and differences between what she terms 'traditional' and 'non-traditional' attitudes.

Associational life is undoubtedly a dominant motif of civil society and is central to the Tocquevillian view of civil society outlined in Chapter 1. Associational life also received systematic empirical investigation in Robert Putnam's *Bowling Alone* (2000) – a work which provoked a central debate in the analysis of how civil society in capitalist societies has changed over time, and potentially experienced an irreversible decline. Much information on associational life can be traced from social surveys. In the United Kingdom, the quantitative evidence in support of an overall decline of participation in formal associations is mixed. But there are strong suggestions that forms of associational life have undergone profound changes in the period between the 1970s and the 21st century. On one hand, evidence points to declining participation in 'traditional' forms of association, especially those linked to working-class institutions; on the other there are indications of new forms of association linked to leisure, consumption and community activism across both rural and urban contexts, and which are increasingly characterised by local-global connectivity. One major body of survey literature argues that social and political participation in Britain has become increasingly stratified along the economic lines as a result of widening income inequality and worsening labour market conditions for working people (Grenier and Wright 2006; Lie et al 2003; Warde et al 2003). Such works emphasise how membership of formal civil society voluntary organisations and political parties is ever more concentrated among the middle and higher social classes whereas the social institutions underpinning working-class forms of participation – mutual aid societies, trade unions, leisure and social clubs – have declined or disappeared. In contrast to both Putnam (1995) and Hall (1999), Grenier and Wright arrive at the following pessimistic conclusion:

> Our analysis suggests a somewhat darker picture. With the withering of many active working class institutions over the past twenty years, formal participation is increasingly concentrated among certain (class-based) groups – those who are active in everything. Its character is becoming increasingly commodified, chosen as a private good and negotiated without personal interaction. (2006: 48)

Examining trends since the 1970s, Savage et al (2009) appear to share this view, pointing to 'a crisis of white, male working class social capital, the ramifications of which are very significant for understanding the contours of social change in Britain' (2009: 71). Their analysis suggests that the decline in working men's participation occurs primarily with regard to trade unions and working men's social clubs. Membership of these organisations, as a proportion of working-class men, has fallen, respectively, from 38.7 per cent and 27.2 per cent in 1972, to 21.7 per cent and 17.7 per cent in 1999. At the same time, they find small increases in membership of sports and hobby clubs, and a more significant increase in membership of professional associations. So, 'traditional' working-class forms of association have declined. But equally the composition of associations has changed to become increasingly 'the province of professional, managerial and white collar workers' (2009: 85). Thus there has been 'a fundamental remaking of the social relationships of associational membership', which are now 'marked by a striking class divide' (2009: 90). Moreover, the extent to which associations are stratified along the lines of class is masked by changes in the nature of participation: from more active and collective to more passive, individualistic and consumer-orientated forms (Cameron 2001; Halpern 2005).

McCulloch (2014) also finds that membership of voluntary associations has declined across age cohorts born between 1955 and 1964, and 1965 and 1974 and argues that this reflects the impact of changing social and economic conditions which influence individual capacity for involvement. For those born before 1954, economic growth and backing from the welfare state enabled working people to accumulate resources that supported participation in collective voluntary associations (2014: 15), whether this be trade unions or new social movements. But by the end of the 20th century, policies designed to increase economic competitiveness – labour market flexibility, deregulation – have had the effect of undermining the habits of sociability and commitment needed for voluntary association (McCulloch 2014). The upshot of this is that formal association may provide a dwindling and more exclusive resource for civil society. However, efforts to quantify the nature and extent of formal associational life are a limited, and potentially misleading, measure of civil society at local levels, and in everyday life. In contrast, and alongside patterns relating to formal association, less formal, and less visible, types of voluntary action remain an extensive feature (McCabe and Phillimore 2018). Moreover, subtler and less visible forms of social action exemplify solidarity and civility in ways which are not captured by the 'sectoral' view of civil society centred on associations (Baumgarten et al 2011; Rucht 2011).

Alongside association, the theme of solidarity, and specifically local collective action and mutual aid, also reflects the close proximity of concepts of community and civil society. Mooney and Fyfe (2006) provide us with one example of this in their analysis of community protests against swimming pool closure in Glasgow; there are numerous cases of similar actions around other public facilities, such as libraries and green spaces which expose the tensions between state and civil society (Hoggett 1997). Hancock et al (2012) argue that actions undertaken in disadvantaged and poor communities in the UK reveal the interface between depoliticised governmental conceptualisations of community, and the more politicised versions of community evident locally. It is important therefore to consider solidarity, as illustrated via community organisation and protest, when making any overall assessments about local civil society. The ongoing nature of action around local community resources will not necessarily be reflected in the measurement of rates of decline in association and participation, especially given the way local voluntary action, self-help and 'below the radar' groups are evolving in the light of transfers of state functions onto communities (Mohan and Mohan 2002; Richardson 2008; Soteri-Proctor et al 2013) and the increasing pressure placed on welfare provision in the context of rising inequality.

Many commentators (Levitas 2004; Amin 2005) have observed that this has not happened in a political vacuum. Firstly, neo-liberalism in the 1980s attacked the post-war society of connections and commitments and state support for community action. Dealing with spatial inequality and levelling-up communities was seen as something that interfered with market efficiency and created dependency. Then came the Third Way, drawing on Hayek, Giddens, Etzioni and Putnam, promoting social cohesion but equally implementing active measures to promote competitiveness through market liberalisation and deregulation. In the UK, this saw New Labour rolling out a range of top-down area-based initiatives such as the New Deal for Communities, Sure Start and Communities First (in Wales), designed to regenerate local areas and build social capital to enable communities to become 'sustainable' (in other words, less reliant on the state). This social-democracy and a mixed economy orthodoxy was challenged in 2010 with the Conservative-Liberal Democrat coalition government's flagship Big Society policy. According to David Cameron, the Big Society would empower individuals, redistribute power to communities and promote a culture of volunteering (Cameron 2010). While many dismissed the concept as nothing more than a cynical attempt to justify austerity and massive cuts in public spending, it fitted with the Conservative's common-sense narrative that the state had become too powerful under New Labour and that individuals and individual communities were best-placed to know what they want and how their needs ought to be met. In the Big Society, individual citizens had a moral obligation to undertake voluntary activity in the community and to take responsibility for their own individual welfare needs (Kisby 2010).

While the Big Society policy withered with increasing austerity, the underpinning principles have remained. With shrunken states, governments in the UK and elsewhere are increasingly looking to draw on people's capacity for association and organisation. For instance, third sector research, and geographical perspectives within this, have examined whether and how voluntary activity becomes embedded in particular places, as well as investigating unevenness in the local and regional distributions of this activity, and the consequences of this for meeting welfare and service needs (Marshall 1997). Such studies indicate how the localisation of voluntary activity converges on poor neighbourhoods of cities, but depends also on the availability of local spaces in which to 'house' such activity (Milligan and Fyfe 2004). According to Milligan and Fyfe (2004) the professionalisation of the third sector has led to its re-territorialising at broader locality scales through formal volunteer centres and larger third sector organisations. Nevertheless third sector research has begun to focus on small locally orientated 'below the radar' voluntary activity (McCabe and Phillimore 2009, Soteri-Proctor et al 2013) pointing to the role of key individuals working at community levels as well as the importance of sites, or hubs, which act as shared spaces for local groups to meet.

Ideas of civility and morality also connect to local social relations and attachments more widely. As Rucht (2011) outlines, the relation of civility to civil society is conveyed in the former's emphasis upon the acceptance of strangers and recognition of the other. The label 'NIMBY' for example has been used *negatively* to characterise some forms of local protest and solidarity against perceived external threats as selfish or parochialist, as if there are automatically 'good' and 'bad' forms of participation. As McLymont and O'Hare (2008) comment, 'such groups are, it is alleged, engaged in an essentially protectionist form of participation that is selfish in ends and uncivil in spirit' (2008: 323). Likewise Meyer and Hyde (2004) highlight 'insular' forms of neighbourhood association in major US cities. Evers (2010: 114) has argued that civility and incivility have been blind spots within research on the third sector and volunteering: 'civility can remind us that civil society is about more than vital associational life and active members' (see also Rucht 2011). Evers' critique returns us to the question of boundaries between civil society, economy and state by questioning how the introduction of market logics and funding streams brings certain kinds of uncivil behaviour into voluntary organisations (2010: 114). This forms just part of the way in which civil society can be taken in hand, and expected to engage with policy development and delivery, or to be orchestrated and managed (Rose 1996; Day 2006a: 242–5). Following this, our own argument here would be to challenge unduly simplistic distinctions between good and bad, civil and uncivil forms.

## Time, place and the un/civil nature of community

A major development within the theorising of local social relations was to introduce the interpretative and symbolic dimensions of community, alongside the extant emphasis on geography and local structural characteristics of places. The emphasis by Cohen (1985) and others on attachment and belonging informed new understandings of community as a mental construct or as existing 'in the mind' (Pahl 2005). Of course, these subjective and symbolic aspects do not exist in isolation from structural and material considerations – they are tied together, through interlocking social relationships of belonging and association. Place continues to matter and have significance because it is within the settings of place that significant relations are formed and maintained. But alongside place, time is also an *enabler* for social relations, 'since it takes time for social contacts to develop and conversely, for community traditions to die out' (Crow and Allan 1995: 152). And also since 'community relationships are patterned over time ... involvement ... is not simply a matter of individual choice' (1995: 156). Crow and Allan make the case for a concept of 'Community Time' which 'shapes and is shaped by the interplay of community as place, social structure and meaning' (1995: 158) and is embedded in the mundane structures and rhythms of everyday life. These points resonate with Crow and Takeda's (2011) description of Pahl's work as 'historically-informed sociological analysis' and their reference to Elias' (1987) critique of the 'retreat of sociologists into the present'.

The alleged incivilities of 'local community' – whether this be the suffocation of insiders or the exclusion of outsiders, and the limitations imposed on both – are connected not only to claims about its spatially but also its temporally bounded nature. Consider, for instance, the following passage from Cresswell (2009: 176, emphasis added):

> The humanistic conception of place, which has been the predominant understanding of place since the 1970s, is simply too fixed, too bounded and *too rooted in the distant past*. As a consequence of these notions of fixity, boundedness, and rootedness, place too often becomes the locus of exclusionary practices. People connect a place with a particular identity and proceed to defend it against the threatening outside with its different identities.

Cresswell's comment elides the theoretical model of place community, the 'humanistic' tradition of academics and social critics, with the actor's model, or view from inside, taken up by community members themselves. But we can note the connection made between an acute orientation to the past (one that is both too rooted and distant) and exclusionary practices, and therefore the 'uncivil'. This appears especially the case when it comes to studies and conceptualisations of the small town and village. For example, the image of rural places as traditional, past-oriented and romanticised, failing to change with the times, and, therefore, as closed to newcomers and outsiders or as harbouring anti-immigrant or racist attitudes. In turn, particular kinds of action within rural civil society become seen as driven towards these ends: maintaining the materialised symbols of the past, and resisting new developments and forms of life (often characterised as 'NIMBYism'). Conversely, civil or progressive notions of community are held to come into fruition where *longstanding* ties and associations have less significance for how people get to belong, thus enabling a more equitable environment for various locals to act together spontaneously. Hence the temporal distinction between the speed and spontaneity of social networks and translocal activism on one hand and the elongated heritage-based community on the other. Stereotypically, virtual networks relate to speed, and conviviality to the present and temporariness, whereas solidarity often rests on individuals with long-established histories of activism and connections to places.

In stark contrast to the overly rooted and fixed conceptualisation of place with which the concept of community is often charged, other ideas have both spatial and temporal connotations of a quite opposite quality. Thus Massey's 'throwntogetherness' has distinct temporal connotations of haste and 'happenstance' (2005: 111), and being assembled hurriedly in small space neighbourly proximities where previous identities have less importance. 'Throwntogetherness' refers to qualities of space produced by previously unrelated trajectories which enables living with difference in close proximity. Similarly, conviviality connotes the productive qualities of fleetingness, brevity and temporariness, although there has also been some recent attention to sustained and deeper forms of conviviality (Wessendorf 2014; Neal et al 2019). This drift might lead to associations of the civil with the urban condition, with major questions marks then left over the relevance of rural and other kinds of sites. It locates civil society as something along the lines of the 'community liberated' hypothesised by urban researchers such as Wellman (1999: 23–8): neighbourly ties which are not overly strong, de-territorialised supportive and enriching networks, with sufficiently large scale to acknowledge diverse ethnic and other identities. This would strongly imply that to choose the small town or rural village as the research site would run counter to the values of civility. In his preface to a classic among Welsh rural community studies (Rees 1975, originally 1950) Carter (1996: 7) sums up later criticism of the rural community as 'an illiberal inhibiting environment' in which the individual is overpowered by the 'smothering constraints of a closed and inward-looking social system'. Whatever claims might be made about village life around civility, friendliness and mutual regard, it would seem that its isolation, closure and lack of privacy means it will always fall short of the ideals associated with civil society.

Temporal representations of community are thus an integral part of the depiction of the scale and spatiality of local civil society: cosmopolitan and convivial civil society as mobile and present and/or future-orientated; uncivil society as parochial, static and local. Such a simplified dichotomy, however, is at odds with both social theorising of time and with the more dynamic and fluid treatments of the community concept. It conforms to the flawed 'ahistorical historicism' challenged by Abrams (1972) in his critique of the way sociology has taken the methodological route to comparison of types, and inferring change between them, rather than actual historical study of action across time. Abrams argues this sets up 'a tendentious relationship between the observable now and a posited unspecific "past"' and provides a rationale for side-stepping 'tedious historical chores' away from 'the need for analyses of structural transition as a temporally and culturally situated process' (1972: 20). Analyses leading to the conclusion of community as 'stuck in the past' can overlook the way time has been theorised, for example by Mead (Mead 1934; Flaherty and Fine 2001) and Adam (1990), in relation to various kinds of social and political projects, which point to the way past, present and future are inter-connected.

According to Adam (1990) the boundary between the present and future is characterised by 'porosity and permeability ... a blurring that makes it almost impossible to establish which time dimension we are dealing with' (1990: 140). While on one hand nostalgia is a preoccupation with the past, it is also future-oriented in its 'concern with something which is about to disappear' (1990: 141). Anderson's (1991) influential concept of 'imagined communities' also drew on a view of community as travelling through time and in which past/present/future are conjoined. Equally, local empirical studies point to considerable nuance in how nostalgia, in both discourse and practice, can have significance for both civil *and* uncivil projects. When linked to meaningful attachments, concerns about aspects of place under threat or disappearing also provide motivation for action and mobilisation in civil society (Tomaney 2013). The 'past' becomes a repertoire, an element of a common stock of knowledge which can be drawn upon for community mobilisation (Roberts 1999: 205). This is evident in urban as well as rural settings. Crehan (2006) provides an example, of a community arts project in East London, where the kind of romantic nostalgia that might easily be refuted with historical facts helps create moments of community experience, with their own generative power, and not necessarily with conservative or nationalistic results. In urban and multicultural contexts, it relates to how contemporary multicultural convivialities may build on histories of openness and porosity which are themselves related to earlier waves of settlement and flow.

Given that the link between nostalgia and uncivil society has been posited most sharply in rural settings, insights from studies such as those of Edmondson (2000), in the rural west of Ireland, are also worth considering here. Building on Crow and Allan's (1994) call for community researchers to pay greater attention to time, Edmondson explores the rural temporal practices in the South Connemara region, contending that nostalgia – defined as a greater affection for past times, or valuing of the past – is not in itself exclusively past-oriented but can include concerns over the future, about succession and the continuity of communal life (see also Adam 1990). Hence what Edmondson refers to as 'communal time' relates to 'productiveness for future life' (2000: 275). Communal time is therefore constituted by attitudes and dispositions about the past, including historical narratives both real and imaginary, which inform action in the present which is geared towards securing the future. In one example discussed by Edmondson, of local action and engagement with authorities concerning the installation of a water pipe (2000: 278), a participant describes the extended length of time that was required for its installation. In this case, communal time was one whereby local action was structured in terms of the ongoing, prolonged, community work of long-term residents, aimed at maintaining social harmony. Whereas for Edmondson nostalgia involves a concern for the future on the horizon, Wheeler's (2017) research with heritage and local history groups in a relatively large village in Norfolk, England presents a challenge to the view that associations emphasising the past are necessarily resistant to change and outside influence. In calling for greater nuance in debates over heritage and exclusion, she suggests scope for progressive local history practices which draw on a sense of continuity with the past.

## Local civil society and comparing communities across time and place

According to Crow (2008), the strengths of community studies lie with their potential to offer a sociology of comparison. That is, the development of accounts which enable comparisons to be made, whether this be between places, and/or over time. Crow lays out three ways through which this commitment to comparison might be upheld: first are research designs involving two or more research sites in which shared conceptual and methodological frameworks can be deployed; second would be to deliberately address time and social change by making links between past and present communities. This can include studies which set out to cross the disciplinary boundaries of history and sociology; as well as those which involving combining of biographical and ethnographic methods, and use of historical archives. The third is the 're-study' where either the same or new researcher(s) revisit the same community, potentially many decades later.

One of the values of bringing time into the equation is to enable distinctions between local contexts to be made *without* resting back on static and mutually exclusive representations. Instead of setting up oppositional types, we may approach this via co-existent, potentially conflicting, social processes of emergence and decline, continuity and discontinuity, of new and older modes of belonging establishing and losing significance. And while these might form the basis for a more nuanced appreciation of community types, they also alert us to reconsider contrasting civil and uncivil narratives of place within the same local field setting.

Two major works in which this comparative value of both past and present perspectives and contrasting research sites is evident are the work of Abrams (Bulmer 1986) and Wallman (1984; 1986) respectively (see Crow and Allan 1994: xviii). In Abrams, we find the historical distinction over time between traditional neighbourhood and modern neighbourhoodism; from Wallman we gain the contrasting types of homogeneous and heterogeneous community. Both contributions provide us with highly fruitful frameworks for theorising change and diversity in local civil society. They are especially important insofar as they suggest continuities, rather than sharp ruptures, between post-structuralist accounts of place and space emphasising openness and heterogeneity and the work of community studies. In emphasising continuity, rather than rupture, we echo critical points made previously by Gans (1992) on 'sociological amnesia' and the drawing of overly sharp theoretical frameworks which impede 'cumulative understanding' (Wilson and Pahl 1988). Again, the aim is not to leave the frameworks and the empirical evidence provided unquestioned, but to illustrate the need to acknowledge both continuity and discontinuity.

## Local civil society in comparative perspective: from neighbourhood to neighbourhoodism

In Abrams' description of 'traditional neighbourhood', we will not find any romanticising of community, nor any positive gloss placed upon it. While it provides us with sources of local civil society in the form of mutual aid and self-help, this is within the context of a highly uncivil society dominated by unemployment, economic adversity, domestic crisis and government disregard (Bulmer 1986: 91–2). In such contexts, people may form themselves into 'communities of the oppressed' (Williams 1973: 131). There were also limits to the extent of mutual aid. That is, there were boundaries as to the giving and receiving. According to Abrams, there is a strong evidence base from historical and social research of what life under traditional neighbourhood was like:

> A densely woven world of kin, neighbours, friends and co-workers, highly localised and strongly caring within the confines of quite tightly defined relationships, above all the relationships of kinship local social networks sufficiently dense, complex and extensive, and evoking sufficient commitment from residents, for a high proportion of local needs for care to be met within. (Bulmer 1986: 91)

What is noteworthy is the historical and spatial patterning of the traditional neighbourhood: this includes historical evidence pointing to its prevalence in mid-19th-century industrial towns and is also evident repeatedly in the famous community studies of the 1950s and in various contexts at this time: East London, rural Wales, North England mining villages. Elements of traditional neighbourhood continued to feature even into the 1980s, and potentially beyond. There is flexibility here as well as scope for continuity and discontinuity. As Bulmer, based on his own research at the time reflects, 'we have come across two, possibly three, localities in which something plainly identifiable as an attenuated version of the traditional neighbourhood system could be recognised' (Bulmer 1986: 91–2).

From the normative civil society viewpoint, traditional neighbourhood is problematic: 'when one considers the social conditions that made it possible one is forced to the conclusion that on balance it is probably rather undesirable' (Bulmer 1986: 92). The significance of this is that we cannot interpret civil society action and the actors (supporting, helping, aiding) outside of the social and economic context which gives rise to these actions. Traditional neighbourhood is indeed 'marked by collective attachment reciprocity and trust' but the contexts were ones of social constraint, isolation and insecurity (Bulmer 1986: 92). The 'helping network' was 'a response to certain highly specified social conditions which one would not wish to see reproduced today' (1986: 92). Unfortunately, all too often, particularly in times of austerity, they are.

Abrams' distinction can be placed in contrast to social theorists who saw the transition from traditional to modern society as lamentable, and in connection with the Durkheimian view of division of labour generating mutual dependencies and bonds. In contrast to traditional neighbourhood, 'modern neighbourhoodism' (1986: 84) is seen as a product of greater geographical mobility, diversity, low-cost state provision. Post-1945, 'the mutual aid born of economic adversity becomes less salient, though in the recession of the early 1980s the pace of change may have slowed down' (1986: 95). This explanation has four key elements: the first two, mobility and choice, anticipate elective belonging. The further two being the formal organisation of welfare and a vastly enlarged sphere of public and political life which takes over from local support and provisioning. Again this raises the possibility that with the withdrawal of welfare or the return of constraints people may need or revert to the older civil aspects.

Overall Abrams contended traditional neighbourhood had 'plainly collapsed ... most choose not to make friends out of their neighbours' (Bulmer 1986: 94). Nevertheless, the distinction Abrams made was one which gave scope for continuities as well. The 'greater mobility and choice' already set in motion by industrialisation – dispersal of kin and friends, commuting, transport, shopping 'reduced the centrality of the neighbourhood as a locus of social interaction and social support' (1986: 94). Yet for some – children, mothers, the elderly, migrants – it remains at the centre of their social world. Thus there is acknowledgement of the survival of some traditional features based on the way close kin continue to provide informal care and support and networks of local information ('namely gossip') sustained within particular socio-spatial settings (1986: 94). Indeed, based on his own extensive community research, Willmott (1986) thought Abrams had over-estimated the degree of change.

Two connections at least here can be made with developments which are often used as the basis of contrast with community studies. One is, as Wellman (1979) found, that the sources of informal social care among friends and family are not necessarily located within the same neighbourhood but are stretched across a broader spatial setting; the other is how online communities can provide forums for 'networks of local information' which help to construct the neighbourhood (for instance, village Facebook sites).

The distinction between traditional neighbourhood and modern neighbourhoodism is not an intrinsically rigid one. In the empirical analysis of particular places, there may be evidence of co-existence at different stages. While both Welsh community studies and research in Bethnal Green are seen as showing the continuation of traditional neighbourhood into the post-war period, a close reading of the texts will also pick up hints of this world being replaced by the modern form. Hence Rees ([1950] 1975) hints at professionalism and formal organisation replacing informal kin ties.

Different civil society elements have different associated temporalities. Mutual aid and support have historical continuities with the traditional neighbourhood; collective action around the neighbourhood not emerging until mid-20th century or later:

> modern neighbourhoodism is in its purest form an attempt by newcomers to create a local social world through political or quasi-political action. Great organisational skills and ingenious organisational devices are often used in attempts to mobilise old and new residents alike in order to protect amenities, enhance resources and, to a greater or lesser [extent] wrench control of the local milieu from outside authorities and vest it in strictly local hands. (Bulmer 1986: 95)

What is striking about Abrams' analysis, is how aspects of contemporary community life which have been asserted as ruptures with the past, can also be viewed as longer term continuities of social change. Modern neighbourhoodism entails 'working out a constructive relationship between the state ... and ... the politicized voice of local attachment' (Bulmer 1986: 95). This is a key shift in local civil society around local civic involvement and the invocation of the neighbourhood as a basis for politics of both intervention and collective action – in the context of threats to amenities and social spaces. The emphasis on collective action is linked to a reconstructive theory of community and place – not as naturals or givens but as a product of the efforts to mobilise attachments to place via collective actions against authorities to protect and enhance assets and resources. This also provides a more complex view of so-called defensive communal responses, which while often characterised as regressive or reactionary are part of how locals take a stand against external developments which objectively or subjectively constitute negative threats to assets which they value. Again, Abrams' comparative framework does not oblige us to presume that the social changes implied through modern neighbourhoodism are any more productive of civil, than they are of uncivil, forms of community relations. Rather this is a question for empirical exploration and the sensitivities of local context.

## Local civil society in comparative perspective: homogeneous and heterogeneous communities

The second comparative model we wish to examine is that of the heterogeneous versus homogeneous community, developed out of Wallman's

(1984) comparative study of two neighbourhood areas in London: Battersea and Bow. While community research based on contrasting research sites can be prone to over-simplification – for example, one place treated as exhibiting one type of community, the other place exhibiting a different type – it is the theoretical contribution of the work, as much as the comparative design, that is of interest. Here the particular insight is not only to describe the open and closed nature of the boundaries, but to link the nature of community to the material resources and constraints which make heterogeneity permissible. Material factors, like housing and labour markets, mean that this type of community is not as voluntary or freely chosen as it would seem, despite the appearance of openness. In understanding Battersea as a community relatively open to newcomers compared to Bow, Wallman states 'housing, jobs and people are mixed and there are so many separate "gates" into local resources that no single group, institution or ideology can claim a controlling share' (1984: 6). Thus what makes the boundaries permeable is 'partly because of the local *tradition* of openness, and partly because local resources allow this to be continued' (1984: 9, emphasis added). We should note that despite the homogenous/heterogenous distinction, both Bow and Battersea are ethnically diverse in composition. Openness, rather, is to do with the ease with which newcomers can become local and belong just like others. In a mixed ethnic area like Battersea, Wallman argued that Black and minority ethnic people could instrumentalise their length of residence in the borough in order to assert their local status, and thereby to trump claims to the contrary based on their immigrant ethnic origin. This claim is, of course, contextual and in other community settings the local/outsider boundary and ethnic boundaries may coalesce and overlap. Battersea has perhaps a peculiar history in terms of its association with progressive politics (Sharpe 2009). In contrast, in Bow, 'residents do not have the same range of choice concerning how they will live' (Wallman 1986: 240): 'Membership in the Bow area, in line with the East End tradition is not so readily achieved' and 'it is generally more difficult to become "local" in the East End than in South London' (1986: 240–1). Indeed, what was potentially crucial about Battersea was that the non-White population was more established: 'By 1978 most of the Caribbean-born had been settled for a generation' (Wallman 1984: 14). Hence the relative openness of the boundary is not just evident in how incomers can become local 'just by moving in' but that they are doing so as a layer on top of previous incomers who have 'stayed around' (Wallman 1986: 240–1).

## Continuities and discontinuities in selected recent local studies

We can further illustrate the benefit of adding time to the analysis by going into some greater detail with Savage et al's (2005) highly influential study of local belonging in Greater Manchester, UK. A key motivation for this work was the problematic significance of place in the context of late capitalist Britain. For some time, the dominant view within sociological and geographical scholarship was that not only could social life no longer be firmly located in particular places within defined boundaries but that identities were also necessarily mobile and transitory, with territory thus replaced by networks and flows. Nevertheless, and despite claims that local identities had lost their significance, Savage et al observe that 'attachment to place remains remarkably obdurate' (2005: 1). Thus, while rejecting an 'outmoded' view of the local as defined in terms of stable face-to-face relationships, they provide us with a prospect of how local belonging may persist via choice and dispositions made available through the effects of globalisation – the global circulation of people, culture and capital – on place. Territory is re-introduced through the embodied nature of dispositions as material sites within everyday life – physical and social spaces. The contemporary significance of local belonging is thus defined by the situated process in which people reflexively make judgements about places – judgements which are themselves related to the richness of globalisation.

Savage et al conducted research in a number of selected residential areas in Manchester – a large 'second tier' metropolitan city – each of which may be characterised as 'loosely middle class neighbourhoods' (Savage et al 2005: 12). They include: suburban estates, gentrified urban working-class housing and an area of rural gentrification (a former mill town 12 miles north of Manchester in the commuter belt which has 'the air of being in the countryside' [2005: 19]). In a sharp break from community studies, which emphasise 'local social relations as defined by those born and bred' (2005: 29), it is incoming social groups who are seen as establishing the dominant place identities and attachments. And the way in which dominant incoming groups *electively* belong to place is the study's key assertion. Their dominance may be due to the economic and civic advantages of incomers compared to locals within the context of prevailing flows of capital and people. The point also needs to be made that this assertion need not be based on a simple opposition between locals and incomers. There is no essential reason why the forms of elective belonging which characterise the local attachments of the incoming groups should be unavailable to those born within the places under study. If nothing else, elective belonging entails a reflexive accounting of how incomers come to live where they do. What incomers do appear to espouse is a relational sense of place which is made meaningful through biographical life history. They bring with them preferences derived from experiences and perspectives accumulated elsewhere.

As mentioned earlier, in Savage et al's view, elective belonging constitutes a break from previous studies in which it was the locally embedded population who were assumed to be the kernel of community (Elias and

Scotson 1965; Strathern 1981). For instance, in Strathern's (1981) study of the village of Elmdon, it is the long-term residents who exercise moral ownership over place, while in the classic study by Elias and Scotson (1965), the 'established' seek to maintain their privileged definition of belonging in the face of challenge from incoming 'outsiders'. In fact, we can see strong continuities between the idea of elective belonging and a rich lineage of investigations of 'insider/outsider' dynamics, not only in the work of Elias and Scotson but also Stacey (1960), Pahl (1965) and Mann (1973), as well as a substantial literature on the effects of migration in rural areas (Boyle and Halfacree 1998). We can also identify threads of openness within empirical studies of the 'suburban' over time. Willmott and Young's (1967) study of suburban life saw districts such as 'Greenleigh' (Redbridge) in outer London as places for mobile populations disaggregated from the inner city to use their movement as an opportunity to adapt working-class identities towards new, 'middle class', patterns of behaviour. Rosser and Harris (1965) and Bell (1968) pursued similar themes in their study of Swansea's social and spatial organisation. As Neal (2016: 66) notes, there are parallels between elective belonging based on neighbourhood in 1990s Manchester, and Wallman's interpretation of the porous boundary in late 1970s Battersea, South London.

This dynamic plays out differently across Savage et al's residential areas, in all of which 'true locals' (sic) formed less than a quarter of the population (2005: 46). In Cheadle, there were virtually no local residents to defer to, but the local versus non-local split was a significant demarcation in Milltown. In Ramsbottom, the gentrified working-class area, there were elements of nostalgia among locals concerning the old industrial base. However, incomers to Ramsbottom did not defer the older residents, but rather regarded them as restricted, blinkered and outdated; longstanding residents were not given moral precedence. There were some similar elements in Wilmslow, where the opinions of 'old blokes' represented those who have 'stayed' (2005: 39). Statements about belonging provided by these locals tended to emphasise being fundamentally of the area (2005: 47) but no longer able to belong fully because the place is not 'their's' any more. In others words, alongside the emergence of electiveness as a dominant form of belonging among the mobile middle class there is a counter-narrative, characterised by decline but nevertheless present, of (self-defined) locals seeing their environments change around them, which connects to arguments made about the social and political attitudes of the 'left behind' (Mann and Fenton 2017: 31–69). This is not to discount the novelty of the idea of elective belonging for capturing contemporary forms of local belonging, but simply to stress the need to trace both continuities and discontinuities across the time and space of local relations. The direction of change – one of elective belonging replacing the established – is not always evident.

Local resident cooperation can be promoted as a continuation of 'who we are'. In an examination of civil society responses to the 2015 refugee crisis across different localities in Wales Guma et al (2019) find that in the case of Aberystwyth the hosting of refugees could be legitimated as part of a shared framing of the town as progressive, international and outward-looking, built in part upon a previous legacy of environmental and peace activism. Of course, this is constrained by, and cannot be separated from either local resistances or the broader national context of anti-migrant discourse. The point, however, is that there is no a priori opposition to make between a global sense of place and a historically grounded, even rooted, local identity in which the past is drawn upon.

As we stated at the outset of this chapter, what these selected studies have to say about relative inclusion and exclusion, and the degree of choice and volition around local membership, provides us with a key connection to the idea of civil society. The uncivil dimensions of the 'East End tradition' of closed local/outsider boundaries, indicated by Wallman's account of Bow, could, for example, be deduced from Dench et al's (2006) re-study of Bethnal Green. While it appears the traditional neighbourhood-based civil society of Willmott and Young 'no longer exists', the picture painted by Dench et al is one of White resentment and racial hostility. However, as Moore points out in his critique of the re-study, there is a more complex reality:

> The East End is not just one story of white resentment and fight against a dying way of life. Whilst there have been serious conflicts between groups within the area, historically the diverse populations have been able to mobilize across internal divisions to oppose fascists in the 1930s, property developers in the 1980s and 1990s and the racism of both the Liberal Democrats who controlled Tower Hamlets from 1986 to 1994 and the British National Party (BNP). Even with a superficial and outsider's knowledge of the complexity of Tower Hamlets it is obvious that a simple division into black and white (or Bangladeshi and white) will not do, nor will ungrounded reports of white resentment. (Moore 2008: 351)

Again, the peculiarities of place matter greatly in the attempt to draw generalisations from the large and diverse body of local studies. Quite different conclusions about multi-ethnicity and local associational life emerge from Charles and Davies' (2005) Swansea re-study. They argue that local associations acted as sites for cross-cutting ties in which 'locals' and post-Second World War Bangladeshi migrants and their descendants got to know one another (2005: 682). Their findings point to the influence of changing dynamics of gender, ethnicity and class: it was women who played a crucial role in local organisations like schools, PTA, Christmas fairs and fundraising activities, while cross-cutting organisations were facilitated by schools and faith-based groups predominantly run by White and Bangladeshi women. In contrast, activities in the Mosque were almost all run by men. At the same time, they found the most extensive range of involvement in associations in their middle-class research site (2005: 686) while they have little to say about men's social clubs and union activity.

If conviviality is to be viewed only in terms of its momentary production in public encounters, then its link to civil society is limited. As Nowicka (2020) highlights, we need to look also at what conviviality omits: 'family, friendship, relations of care and intimacy' among other things (2020: 17). Countering some claims as to the fleetingness of conviviality, Neal et al (2019) argue for putting conviviality into dialogue with community. Drawing on fieldwork in three different urban settings, they find how social leisure associations (running groups, coffee mornings, gardening groups) act as contexts for the 'elective coming together of often ethnically diverse others' (2018: 69). As an established pattern of both disposition and interaction, conviviality enables the settlement and sense of belonging of diverse newcomers. Wessendorf (2014) also acknowledges that conviviality can take on a more communal, durable and sustained form via what Lofland (1989) describes as 'the parochial realm' of clubs and associations. In line with what Charles and Davies found in their research into Swansea, this resonates with concerns about how civil society 'thickens' and the importance of associational life for social capital. Associations also feature centrally within Pahl's (1996) reconstructive work on community, citing in particular the 'communities of association' favoured by 'comfortable England': local arts festivals, tidying-up schemes, the cultivating of local heritage and hobby and leisure groups. The recognition of the scope for *sustained* and *durable* civil interactions has led recent work to re-engage continually with, rather than draw a sharp distinction from, the concept of community. The emphasis on association, in turn, links to the shift to a more voluntary and open community concept. Thus 'whereas community life in the past was imposed on people, being largely based on involuntary relationships. Now, people choose their associates, and, perhaps more importantly, choose with whom not to associate' (Pahl 1996: 91). It certainly resonates with anthropological approaches (Amit and Rapport 2002) which demonstrate how various 'real' communities are never the homogeneous, exclusive or geographically bounded units they are assumed to be within the popular and political imagination.

## Conclusion

We began this chapter by suggesting that local civil society can be seen to consist of three main building blocks – association, solidarity and civility, with civility perhaps representing the most elemental of these. The persistent richness of informal associational life in studies across space, and over time, should certainly encourage further critical reflection on those negative assessments of civil society which have too often been over-reliant on quantitative measures of formal participation. Moreover, in local studies we can see how these three elements are inter-twined in varying ways, and that this is a matter for empirical investigation. Many of the previous studies discussed here indicate a close relationship between association and civility, whereby everyday associations act as important spaces for the generation of the latter, as has been indicated by current approaches to conviviality. Based on this point alone we would argue that local studies provide a valuable avenue for exploring and theorising further the links between the association-based conceptions of civil society and ideas of civility (Rucht 2011). While conviviality can be inferred to connote civility in contexts with high levels of diversity and mobility, there are other contexts, including those tied to indigenous communities where solidarity and justice depend on elements of closure, and require familiarity with and adaptation to pre-existing communities. Georgiou (2017) for instance, also on the basis of neighbourhood research in London, has challenged the assumption that 'convivial open-ness in itself is enabling of a political commitment to equality and justice' – the latter requires not just everyday civility but solidarity (2017: 266).

We then examined time and its relations to community, and how the civil/uncivil dimensions can be traced to different temporal practices. for example, the uncivil viewed as 'stuck in the past' or as excluding those with little or no historical connection to place, and thereby the civil as framed around choice and freedoms of newcomers and locals alike to get involved (or not). Put simply, the investigation of local civil society is intimately connected to debates concerning community as both spatially and temporally bounded. Following on from this, we considered ways in which these distinctions are drawn in local studies across rural and urban settings. One of the benefits of bringing time into the equation is to enable distinctions to be made without falling back on static and mutually exclusive representations. Instead of setting up oppositional types, we can envisage co-existent, potentially conflicting, social processes of emergence and decline, continuity and discontinuity, of new and older modes of belonging establishing and losing significance. And while these might form the basis for a more nuanced appreciation of community types, they also alert us to reconsider contrasting narratives of place within the same local field setting. Any place-based study would need to contend with the rival versions and respective counter-narratives put forward by different residents.

# 3

# Uncovering local civil society in two Welsh villages

The evidence in this book comes from the study of two villages in North East Wales. The choice of 'village' as a focus for a study of local civil society occurs at a time when many observe how modern life is increasingly mobile and subject to change. In such a context it might be argued that the traditional view of 'the village' as a close-knit community with deeply rooted bonds has become less interesting, as people within them have decreasing ties and commitment to place. As such it may seem that villages have little to tell us about wider developments in society and civil society in particular. Unsurprisingly, we take the opposing view that villages provide a unit of study that remains relevant in reflecting upon how the structures and practices of local civil society have changed, and are changing. Interest in villages and village life is a well-established theme among rural sociologists, anthropologists and social geographers. Their work has produced numerous individual case studies of village structure and social relations (for instance Williams 1956; Littlejohn 1963; Blythe 1969) often referred to as 'community studies'. While these have been idiosyncratic both in approach and analysis, efforts have been made in theoretical reviews to bring them together, draw out their lessons and reach some general conclusions (Frankenberg 1969; Bell and Newby 1971; Harper 1989). Others have sought to produce classifications of different types of villages and their social natures and implications (Pahl 1968; Newby 1980; Harper 1989; Murdoch and Marsden 1994). Villages have been used quite widely as sites for comparative analysis around specific questions of development and change in the countryside (Cloke et al 1997) while others have immersed themselves in village life to carry out detailed ethnographic investigations (Rapport 1993; Bell 1994).

In Britain, much of this work has focused on the particular paradigm of the English village and its social and material characteristics, which has entered into both academic discourse and a vast body of literary and other cultural explorations (see Bell 1994: 90). The idea of the quintessential village and its typical social and physical features has penetrated strongly into the popular imagination and influenced people's choices of lifestyles and aspirations. Particular examples and images have become embedded in distinctions between town and country, rural and urban, to form a key ingredient of ideas of a 'rural idyll' (Newby 1980). Contrary to what some of those images might suggest, recent research has seen the emergence of what we might call the standard model of a modern English village, as a place of ethnic homogeneity and class diversity, while the impact of forces like social and geographical mobility, counter-urbanisation, and changes in patterns of work and leisure have made villages useful places in which to observe the playing out of relationships of class, gender and social diversity within a relatively intimate setting.

In some respects, villages are like any other place. While often bounded, their boundaries are rarely hard and fast, they can be isolated but not self-contained, and while they may contain dense social networks and family relationships, most have experienced flux, and reflect the dynamism of wider society. For our purposes, comparisons between the rural and urban are not important, nor do we subscribe to a romantic uniqueness of social solidarity and coherence often ascribed to villages. What the village does offer to us is a particular scale of space and spatial context that lends itself to the study of local civil society. That is not to say that villages do not have interesting and sometimes unique attributes that contribute to the formation of local civil society. The fluidity of social relations within a village can be more overt – lacking the cloak of anonymity found in more urban spaces – so lending itself to observation and investigation. Villages are often shaped more clearly by their histories than the 'neighbourhoods' that are often their urban equivalent. This in turn, can define how they relate to and integrate with 'outside' institutions including larger civil society structures, the state and the market. Furthermore, increases in migration, and the factors of inclusion and exclusion in villages commonly result in 'belonging' constantly being defined and redefined with consequences for local association. We argue therefore that the village provides both a convenient and an interesting space for observing, recording and analysing how people act together within associational forms, groups, organisations and activities that form a local civil society.

## The 'village' as local civil society

Many early studies of villages – particularly those produced in Wales – were arguably examinations of rural life and culture rather than theoretically driven studies. While ground-breaking at the time in following an anthropological approach to the study of Western rural life, they rarely contained references to sociological perspectives and concepts. Consequently the studies often give the appearance of simple, descriptive accounts (Day 1998b), and the rationale for the use of the village as the focus of study is not always given. For example, the founding Welsh rural community study, *Life in a Welsh Countryside* by Alwyn Rees (1950) examined the Montgomeryshire parish of Llanfihangel-yng-Ngwynfa. According to one of his contemporaries, (Owen 1986: 28) Rees had 'no particular methodological approach in mind'. The place which he describes – while typical of many in rural Wales – was not the centralised village settlement more typically described in England, but a loosely bounded patchwork of houses and farms spread across an ill-defined geographical space. According to Rees (1950) the area contained a web of social relationships based more around family and religion than place. Yet that is not to say that Rees was not interested in local civil society. He argued that life in Llanfihangel actually thrived on the absence of an organising centre, displaying a social organisation in which funerals, weddings and gatherings around 'hearth and home' were more important than formal associations in bringing people together.

According to Owen (1986: 34), Rees' study, as planned in 1938 was intended to be the first in a series of such studies of selected rural communities in various parts of Wales. The scheme was delayed by the war, and further studies were not subsequently published until the 1960s. Lewis (1986) records investigations of 11 such 'communities' in North and West Wales between 1940 and 1968. Four studies appeared in the volume *Welsh Rural Communities* (Davies and Rees 1960) all dealing with populations of between one and two thousand, but not necessarily designated as 'villages'. Two of the studies deal with the functions of a rural neighbourhood and a small market town. T. Jones-Hughes' contribution on Aberdaron, situated at the tip of the Llyn peninsula was subtitled 'The social geography of a small region' while Emrys Jones' chapter dealt with the town of Tregaron in central Cardiganshire. Trefor Owen examined the social life of the village of Glan-llyn which in 1949 he described as taking place predominantly in the 15 small neighbourhood chapels (there was one chapel for every 63 inhabitants) drawing parallels with puritanical Hebridean communities that he had studied previously (Owen 1956). The theme of religiosity and existence of a nonconformist charter that saw no difference between the sacred and secular can be found in many post-war studies of rural Wales, including David Jenkins' chapter on Aber-porth. In a later study of south Cardiganshire (Jenkins 1971: 6) Jenkins adopts the terminology of 'parish' for what he defines as 'a land of dispersed farms and small villages'. He describes an area within which he contends it is not possible to draw strict boundaries around communities as might be done 'if settlements were nucleated in villages with open countryside between them'. He is nevertheless prepared to call the whole area a community (1971: 20).

In what has been described as 'the seminal anthropological study of a mainland British rural community' (Cohen 2005) Frankenberg (1957) nails his colours to the mast when he labels his chosen locality as a *Village on the Border*. Glynceiriog, hidden under the pseudonym of 'Pentrediwaith' or 'place without work', pointing to the fact that the community had lost the economic basis of its existence when its slate quarries were closed before the Second World War, is identified as a civil parish in a North Wales valley, a compact geographical unit, and a community.

Frankenberg's analysis concentrates on the 600 or so inhabitants of 'Pentre'; the remainder of the 1,000 who live in the parish occupy one other small 'hamlet', and several clusters of houses and farmsteads. His investigations were more theoretically driven than those of many of his predecessors. Influenced by the conflict-oriented Manchester anthropology of Max Gluckman, Frankenberg observes how a false impression of consensus and harmony was presented in 'Pentre', concealing conflict and division as a significant driving force within the community. He also insists that the apparent isolation of this 'village' and its 'villagers' is an illusion, since 'geographically, economically and historically, the village is part of a larger whole' (Frankenberg 1957: 9). Studying a village with a known history and environment also enabled Frankenberg to dispense with much of the introductory material on ecology and general background that was usually presented in anthropological reports (Owen 1986: 42). Glynceiriog is located only a dozen miles from our own study area, and we are happy to follow Frankenberg's example, both in referring to our study sites as villages, and in stressing that on our part this does not signify any presumption of closure, boundedness, or inwardness. These indeed are issues that we want to explore.

While the focus of these Welsh studies may be different, in common the village is viewed as somewhere where community and place are isomorphic. Identifying community in 'place' meant understanding those places holistically through various forms of ethnography. Accounts and reports were organised into varying spheres of life – for example family/ domesticity, work, association, religion, language and leisure. Distinction and elaboration of each of these spheres was necessary to understand the whole, and the nature of community rested to a large extent on how these spheres overlapped with each other and mapped on to the boundaries of specific places. Too much overlap between spheres of family, work and leisure was a recipe for exclusion of outsiders; too little overlap had implications for work-life balance, restricting time opportunities for social participation in place.

At the time the early accounts of rural community were often viewed as overly descriptive and static, but recent reflections of these studies are more balanced, and emphasise their relative merits for understanding the local effects of social change, and their methodological contributions. Later studies such as Frankenberg's also challenged the image portrayed by Rees of villages as wholly 'organic', closed and totalising. Despite many communities presenting themselves as such, the reality was very different and communities were 'alive to the differences between people, adaptable to change, and capable of accommodating divergent, as well as shared, identities' (Day 1998b: 258). Nonetheless, what many village studies capture is the fundamental social process of relationality through forms of belonging and 'place-attachment'. Like Frankenberg (1957), at about the same time, though at the opposite end of the country, another major contribution to our understanding of Welsh communities (Williams 1960) drew on a personal experience of growing up in what the author referred to as 'border country', namely those parts of Wales which lie close to the boundary with England. Williams described the immediacy and directness of relationships within what he termed the 'knowable community' (Williams 1973: 23).

In common with such earlier work, later social anthropologists such as Cohen (1982) have identified the distinctive close social association found in isolated rural communities that were formed of kinship, work, class, neighbourhood and religion, producing a social integrity and a political solidarity against the outside world that was often perceived as unique.

'Place-attachment' refers to the generally emotional bonds that people develop with places, usually resultant of factors such as residence length and social ties, but also influenced by physical features and symbolic meanings such as those related to a place's history (Low and Altman 1992). Accordingly, mobility and 'place attachment' are often seen as incompatible, and as two extremes of a continuum (Gustafson 2014). Most studies find that place attachment increases with length of residence (Brehm et al 2006) and therefore will inevitably be undermined by what Urry (2000: 186) describes as global 'networks and flows' that weaken endogenous social structures such as the village. Under such pressures and divorced from their agrarian or industrial origins, it is argued that villages become unable to reproduce the structures that once made them relevant. In Wales, Day (2006b) agrees, describing rural Welsh villages as 'remarkable social creations' of their time, but of which there is now little left of the identity or community they engendered. Following this argument, those living in villages now lead more isolated lives and forge identities and belong to communities that are increasingly detached from the places in which they live, as mobile people become 'liberated from place' (Lewicka 2005). According to Day (1998b: 247), this was particularly marked in rural Wales, where outward migration, accompanied by a counteracting inward movement of predominantly urban emigres, came mostly from across the English border.

In this context it might seem that there is decreasing relevance in studying 'the village' yet, we argue that the very reasons why villages are perceived to be less important in an increasingly mobile and global world are the reasons why we choose to do so. Contrary to such claims, there is some evidence that the decline of the village is not inevitable, and while the overall intensity of the attachment to a village has diminished over the years, a 're-discovery of place' may be occurring (Lewicka 2005: 382). As Milbourne and Kitchen found in their study of rural Wales (2014), increased mobility does not necessarily prevent villagers from developing a meaningful relationship with their place of residence, and may even encourage them to do so. They found that rural places provide important spatial moorings for residents, associated with senses of belonging, tradition and stasis. Indeed, one of the main reasons why people remain in these types of rural locality in the face of the withdrawal of local services is the strength of their attachment to place (2014: 335).

Here, it is helpful to consider Pahl's (1966) studies of semi-rural villages in England where similar large-scale population shifts took place in the latter part of the 20th century. While this movement inevitably changed the distinctiveness of many rural communities, Pahl observed how some villages changed and became 'villages of the mind' as middle-class urbanites moved to the countryside and through engaging in local society re-created the cultural and social structures that they 'imagined' existed previously, while simultaneously substituting the actual realities:

> The middle class people come into rural areas in search of a meaningful community and by their presence help to destroy whatever community was there. Part of the basis of the local village community was the sharing of the deprivations due to the isolation of country life and the sharing of the limited world of the families within the village. The middle class try to get the cosiness of village life, without suffering any of the deprivations, and while maintaining a whole range of contacts outside. (Pahl 1966: 9)

This idealised version of place was revisited by Savage (2008) whose focus was on how the middle class claim belonging as a result of their choice to move to an area that holds functional and symbolic importance for them, and subsequently project moral ownership over the place where they live. Benson and Jackson (2013) go further in their investigation of how the more mobile middle classes seek to 'practice' place-maintenance in village settings as a way of maintaining moral ownership and find that while the place-attachment found in villages may be different, it still resonates in a globally mobile world. While most villages are not the culturally and socially homogenous places of the past, unlike cities, where social differentiation provides an inexhaustibility of human relations with endless cultural and social possibilities, villages are still often places where face-to-face contact engenders mutual understanding and group identification. This in turn can maintain local civil society, and under certain conditions, create the possibility for new groups to form or emerge around specific interests.

We have therefore conflicting views of 'the village' and what villages have become, but they retain relevance as a unit of study in contributing to our understanding of other communities and wider civil society. Like Frankenberg (1957), in his work on Glyn Ceiriog, or Emmet in her study of identity in Llanfrothen (Emmett 1964) we do not observe 'the village' as a social and cultural isolate, but attempt to explain its dominant social configurations within the social and economic context of Britain as a whole.

## A tale of two villages

In this section we present a range of evidence on our study sites. Both are in North East Wales in the United Kingdom and while contrasting, have common frames of reference. We selected the first study site based on well-documented evidence of a rich history and contribution to Welsh civic life. The second was selected some time later for contrasting features. We were encouraged to do so by one of our respondents – a local politician – who remarked on 'unusual' levels of voluntary activity and participation in the village. We made a number of visits and examined administrative data to uncover a site that in many ways provided a foil to contextualise the emerging findings from our first site. There were also analytical and pragmatic factors in our site selection – such as relative proximity of both to our research base – and as places where as researchers, we had some prior knowledge and personal contacts that provided essential gateways into each community. In describing them we focus on the structural contexts and social processes that the literature and our own evidence suggests are important in relating the concepts of place, space and time to local civil society.

First, we examine the *contextual* factors that characterise the environment of the village and therefore its inhabitants. This includes elements of geography and history, but also incorporates variables such as the size of community and regional influences. Second, we examine a range of social and economic indicators that might help in understanding how the homogeneity of social class and class cultures might be important. Finally, we present data that might be described as *situational*. This is to do with the actual and symbolic interactions that take place between individuals and how they might relate to the rootedness of local civil society. This is allied to Cornwall's (2002) concept of 'situated practice' where the places and spaces in which civil society takes place are framed 'with reference to actual political, social, cultural and historical possibilities' (Cornwall 2002). Viewing civil society as 'situated' suggests that places that are superficially similar may produce patterns of involvement that are quite different, requiring a more in-depth exploration of places to fully understand how spaces are opened, or filled. In the 'village' literature, this has particular resonance. For example, the villagers studied by Frankenberg (1957) in his ethnography of Glyn Ceiriog (see Figure 3.1) considered themselves a united community, bound together by kinship and acquaintanceship and common isolation. What he concluded from his research, however, was that the community was deeply divided. As Iris Young argues, while communities are often portrayed as models of face-to-face relations, 'the desire for community relies on the same desire for social

**Figure 3.1:** Location map showing our two study sites with the large town of Wrexham and Glyn Ceiriog, the site of Frankenberg's study (1957)

wholeness and identification that underlies racism and ethnic chauvinism, on the one hand, and political sectarianism on the other (Young 1986: 2).

## Contextual factors

Our first study site is the large village of Rhosllanerchrugog (more commonly referred to colloquially as 'Rhos' or 'the Rhos') with a population of 9,694 (Office for National Statistics [ONS] 2011a) some six miles from the large town of Wrexham. Our second site, just seven miles away is the smaller village of Overton-on-Dee (Overton) which at the 2011 Census had a total population of 1,988. Both are located in Wales, a country that is part of the United Kingdom, bordered by England to the east and the Irish Sea to the west. Wales was conquered by the English in 1282 and since then has shared much of its political and social history with the rest of Great Britain. While a majority of the population in most areas speak English as a first language, Welsh is the joint official language and spoken by around 20 per cent of the population (ONS 2011a). As one of the four nations which comprise the United Kingdom, Wales retains a distinct social, political and cultural identity, and since 1998 has held devolved powers of government in a number of areas including agriculture, economic development, education, health, housing, local government, social services, tourism, transport and the Welsh language. Previously exercised by the National Assembly for Wales, these powers are now vested in the Welsh Parliament or *Senedd* based in Cardiff.

Both of our study villages lie within the boundaries of the County Borough of Wrexham, one of 22 local authority areas within Wales. Yet despite proximity, the villages have followed very different trajectories, the consequences of which are manifest today. Both villages are located in an area known since medieval times as the *Maelor*, the Welsh land bordering England and spanning the River Dee which flows from the hills of Snowdonia in North Wales to the Roman city of Chester, and then on to the Irish Sea.

The *Maelor* was divided in the 13th century into the *Welsh Maelor* – the land to the west of the river – and the *English Maelor* – the lands to the east (Davies 2007). The two areas remained administratively separate until they were brought together within Wrexham Maelor District Council in 1974.

## History

The history of our first village, Rhosllanerchrugog, has been well-documented by a number of scholars of industrial history. Considerable literature therefore exists relating to both the industries and the unique collective social and civic life of the village that industry created. Rich sources also include the *Rhos Herald*, a local paper published between 1894 and 1966, and *Nene*, the Welsh-language community paper (*Papur Bro*[1]) which is still published monthly.

Prior to the late 18th century, the area was small collection of isolated farmsteads and cottages on the edge of moorland known as Llanerchrugog within the *Welsh Maelor* (Laidlaw 1995). The development of the present-day settlement can be attributed largely to the north-east-Wales coal seam that passes under the hill upon which it sits. During the first stage of industrialisation the community of 'Rhos' sprang up among the open-cast pits or drifts which mined the outcrops of coal on the moorland edge. Inhabitants constructed their own houses, either by encroaching on common land as squatters or by paying a nominal rent to a ground landlord. Rhos continued to expand during the 19th century from a community of 1,244 residents in 1811, to 3,467 by 1841 and over 9,000 residents by 1901 (Dodd 1971).

Unlike the industrial villages of South Wales which drew labour from not only rural south and mid-Wales but from across the United Kingdom and Ireland, much of the population of Rhos originated from the upland farming communities of North West Wales. Their migration was prompted by the enclosure of common land which deprived many small farmers of their livelihoods and the agricultural depression after the Napoleonic wars. The immigrants retained their native tongue and the village of Rhos became and remained to a large extent, a close – and some might say closed – Welsh-speaking community in an area near to the border where English was more commonly spoken (Dodd 1971).

The village was noted as being self-sufficient from its beginnings with a tradition of self-government and nonconformism before it was eventually taken under administrative control by a newly formed Wrexham Rural District Council and provided with its own Parish Council in 1894. However, in the earlier nascent civil society, local traditions and the living conditions did not necessarily meet the expectations of Victorian society. Some 19th-century observers were shocked at the appalling conditions which prevailed in Rhos and were virtually unanimous in describing the villagers as 'the architects of their own dwellings, the authors of their own misfortunes' (Ingen et al 1848). A sub-commissioner for the 1847 Welsh Education Commission (the Blue Books[2]), condemned the dwellings and the degraded habits of the villagers who inhabited them. He beheld Rhos and declared that 'nothing could more forcibly illustrate the imperfect nature of indigenous civilisation if isolated and unaided' (Laidlaw 1995). Observers also commented on the threat to public order represented by such large bodies of population 'living outside the supervision of a squire or master' (Rogers 1963). The early miners of Rhos expressed their independence by taking a leading part in the sometimes riotous labour struggles of the 1830s. The most famous episode in this struggle – 'the Battle of Cinder Hill' – saw a confrontation between striking miners and their families and yeoman cavalry taking place within the village. The nonconformism of the residents of Rhos was religious as well as civic. Evangelical Protestantism was embraced in Rhos and during the 19th century, the many chapels won large numbers of converts who, according to Rogers, successfully inculcated the virtues of temperance, thrift and obedience. The Welsh Religious Revival of 1904 had a further impact on Rhos. The famous bardic line '*Beibl a Rhaw i Bobl y Rhos*' ('a Bible and a Spade for the People of Rhos') reflects the importance of both coal-mining and the chapels on the village's culture and heritage (Portmadog-Jones 1981).

Such virtues instilled a degree of ambition among the residents, many of whom had aspirations to rise above the cultural poverty of working-class provincial life. In the late 19th and into the 20th century Rhos, like many other industrial villages, had a vivid associational life with many organisations whose memberships were often based on social networks anchored in the chapels and whose worthy aims were derived from the ethical teachings preached there. Many of the Rhos chapels supported choirs, concert parties, drama and debating societies. In a similar way, the village's pubs, which had a vigorous social life of their own, mobilised their supporters into sports teams (Laidlaw 1995).

The existence in Rhos of a strong ethos of participation in local civil society with a community characterised by dense social networks is not surprising. Frankenberg's study of nearby Glyn Ceiriog indicated that the basic building blocks of organised associations tended not to be individuals but informal associations of three to six villagers who joined, participated and withdrew from voluntary organisations as groups (1957: 117). Rhos frequently saw the duplication of similar organisations over a small area, as neighbourhoods vied with each other. In some cases this was territorial, in others related to allegiance to one of the 20 or so nonconformist chapels or the many pubs. Existing social institutions often gave birth to others as people known to each other through these contexts mobilised using existing social networks to organise other activities. These bodies were often explicitly associated with their parent body and regarded its members as being under an obligation to support the new enterprise. Yet as well as uniting local society, voluntary organisations often divided it. Intense association, shared ambitions and, in the case of the musical associations, familiarity with an arcane terminology meant that voluntary organisations could constitute an exclusive society even in the heart of the densest working-class community. Laidlaw (1995: 104) quotes one local author observing that: 'If there was ever a mafia in Wales they would surely consist of Male Voice Choristers.' Meanwhile, the *Rhos Herald* noted in 1938 that obtaining 'complete unity in any Rhos movement is extremely difficult' and referred to the long history of splits and secessions in the village's chapels and choirs.

Many commentators cite the Rhos Miner's Institute as representative of the community's ambition to prove, and improve itself. The Stiwt, as it became known, was far grander than buildings with similar functions in other mining villages. The neo-classical style aped that used in official buildings and the Institute clock marked the hours with the Westminster chimes. It housed a 490-seat proscenium arch theatre, along with rehearsal spaces, meeting and reading rooms – but notably, no bar serving alcohol. The building was constructed with funds raised by the community at large, but it was the active 'respectable' elements of the community who determined that it should represent the highest aspirations of the village rather than seeking to provide for baser tastes. Over time, it also came to define the village itself and even today, people say that to call yourself a resident of Rhos you must have been born within sight of the Stiwt clocktower.

As with many other villages that grew out of the industrial revolution, Rhos' fate was inextricably linked to local and global demand for mineral resources, and the 20th century saw a long decline that ultimately ended with the cessation of mining in North East Wales in the 1980s. The fate of the Stiwt perhaps best reflects the trajectory that the village has taken, with a slow decline after the war that eventually saw it closed in 1977. Yet fully aware of its status in reflecting Rhos' unique cultural heritage, a 'Save the Stiwt' campaign started in 1978 and quickly raised enough funds to re-open the building. As part of the campaign a play was performed based on themes suggested by reminiscences of local life performed by musicians and actors who had originated in Rhos along with over 300 local people. Such nostalgia is still evident in regular exhibitions, performances and talks in the Stiwt that maintain a narrative and self-image of successful local voluntary associations and chapel values which give Rhos a singular atmosphere which in turn imparts a unique legacy to its most famous children (Laidlaw 1995). Nonetheless, that the population of Rhos has remained stable for a century suggests a kind of stasis over that period despite significant economic and social change.

Our second village, Overton-on-Dee, lies on the edge of an escarpment that winds its way around the course of the River Dee, from which its name is derived. For most of its history the village was an exclave of the traditional county of Flintshire known as *Maelor Saesneg* (the English *Maelor*). As an exclave it is surrounded on three sides by the English counties of Cheshire and Shropshire, but its Welsh roots can be traced back to the 12th century when a castle was built by Madog ap Maredudd, a prince of Powys. Nonetheless, as a village on the border, identities are inevitably fractious and as far back as 1887, at a Boundary Commission inquiry in Overton, it was found that most of the population of the area favoured it becoming part of Shropshire, in England.

Not much is known about Overton until in 1279 when Edward I granted Robert de Crevequer the right to hold a weekly market and an annual fair in what was referred to as a town, and seven years later the king granted Overton to his wife, Eleanor. It was created a free borough by royal charter in 1292 when '56 taxpayers dwelled here', a reasonable proportion of them probably of Welsh extraction (Clwyd Powys Archaeological Trust n.d.). The town was sacked and burnt by Madog ap Llywelyn during his revolt against the English in 1294, and again in 1403 was razed by Owain Glyndwr (the last native Welshman to hold the title Prince of Wales) leading to the general abandonment of the town. In the 1530s John Leland noted there were 'not twenty houses' in the town. However, despite the assumed reduction in population, Overton retained its market through until the 19th century, and was effectively the secular centre of Maelor Saesneg. Into the 20th century the village and much of the surrounding area was owned by the Bryn-y-Pys Estate whose proprietor was entitled to a Parliamentary seat. Bryn-y-Pys Hall was built in the 1500s and was bought by Edmund Ethelston Peel in 1850. Peel was the eldest son of the Rev. Charles Wicksted-Ethelston of Wicksted Hall, Cheshire, who married Anne Peel, cousin of The Rt Hon Robert Peel – British Prime Minister between 1834 and 1835 and 1841 and 1846. The estate remains in the same family today (Coflein 2020).

In the centre of the village are a number of historic buildings focused around the Anglican Church of St Mary the Virgin in whose churchyard are several famous yew trees of which the oldest may be more than two thousand years old (Done and Williams 1992). As well as some fine, large historic houses the village contains a row of almshouses and a number of half-timbered cottages, many dating back to the 17th century. Of particular interest is the 19th-century 'Cocoa and Reading Rooms', a community building from 1890 provided to foster temperance. Away from the main streets, there has been a significant amount of peripheral development including small estates of social housing – although many homes are now owner-occupied – a development of housing for older people, and plenty of modern detached and semi-detached houses and bungalows.

Overton might be described as a 'closed' settlement, the product of the 'estate system' where there was monopoly holding of landed property. In such circumstances development was relatively more prescribed and contained, life more regulated and the social economy more narrowly agrarian in its focus. This is in contrast to 'open' settlements – like Rhos – where property holding was more dispersed, development less restricted, life less controlled and the social economy more dynamic, more diverse and expansive (Jackson 2012). The open/closed distinction used by rural historians such as Mills (1973) has a bearing not only on how villages developed, but on the civil relations found therein. For example, it can be used to interpret patterns of religious adherence where in closed settlements, under supervision of the landowner, there would be greater attendance at Anglican places of worship and less dissent in the form of nonconformism. While not deterministic, the open/closed binary has been shown to have some utility into the late 20th-century. Short (1992) focuses on analysing the longer-term development of settlement form, examining how social structure and class relations are still affected by the historic legacy of open/closed settlements. In general, the centralised land ownership of closed villages, along with the impact of middle-class migrants and their imaginings of rural idyll, has resulted in less new development,[3] and it is argued that in places such as Overton, the 'estate' continues to act as a social and cultural check on the rate and nature of local change.

## Socio-economic profiles

It is clear that each village in our study has its own distinct history and characteristics, yet we also selected them expecting them to have residents with differing stocks of economic and cultural capital and therefore distinctive local civil societies. We examined data from the most recent UK Census (ONS 2011a) along with a number of other UK and Welsh Government sources to provide a broad perspective within which our ethnography can be positioned.

First, the age-profiles of the two villages are distinct (Figure 3.2). While both villages have similar proportions of children and young people, Rhos has a slightly higher proportion of younger adults, while there are more older adults in Overton. Neither village, however, differs markedly (+/-3 per cent) from the age-profiles across Wales as a whole.

In Figure 3.3 we observe some differences in the marital and partnership status of residents, with more single people in Rhos and more married couples in Overton. The divorce rates in Rhos are average for Wales but are higher than average in Overton. Looking at families with dependent children, the proportions led by a lone parent are similar in Rhos and Overton, but in Rhos, more parents cohabit, while in Overton marginally more children are in families where parents are married.

**Figure 3.2:** Age by single year (combined)

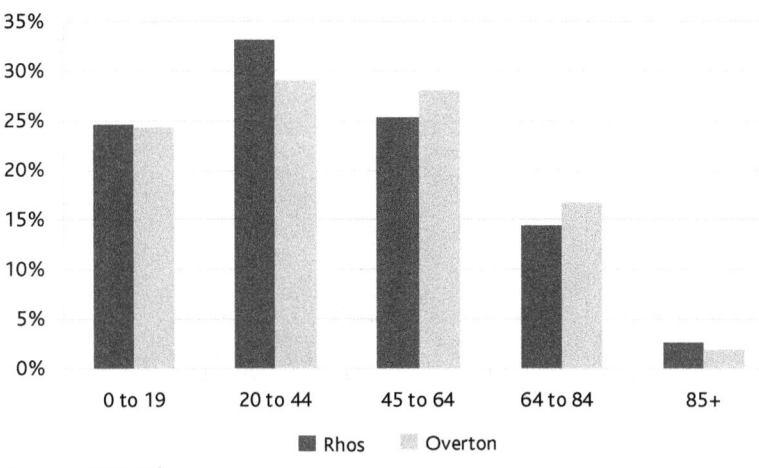

Source: ONS 2011b

**Figure 3.3:** Marital and civil partnership status

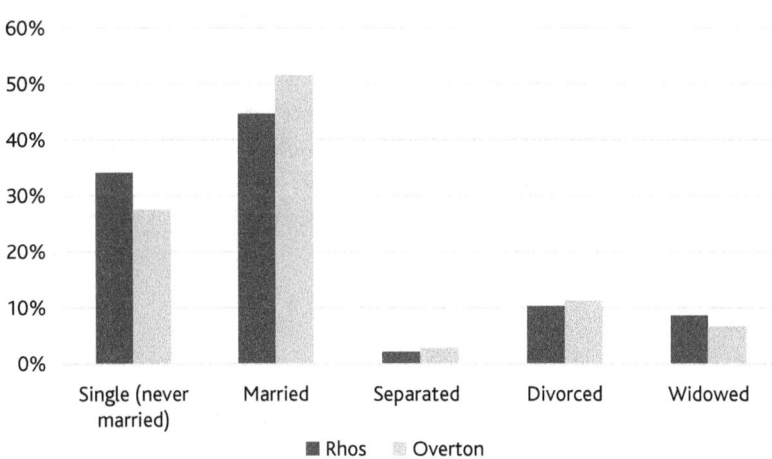

Source: ONS 2011b

The differences in occupations in Rhos and Overton suggest a significant gulf in potential household incomes and therefore economic capital (Figure 3.4).

This is consistent with the ACORN classification[4] for the villages. ACORN classifies neighbourhoods on a scale of between 1 and 59, with 1 being 'affluent achievers' and 59 being 'urban adversity'. The average score for Overton postcodes is 18 ('rising prosperity'), whereas the average in Rhos is 38 ('financially stretched'). ACORN also provides descriptive categories

**Figure 3.4**: Residents' occupations

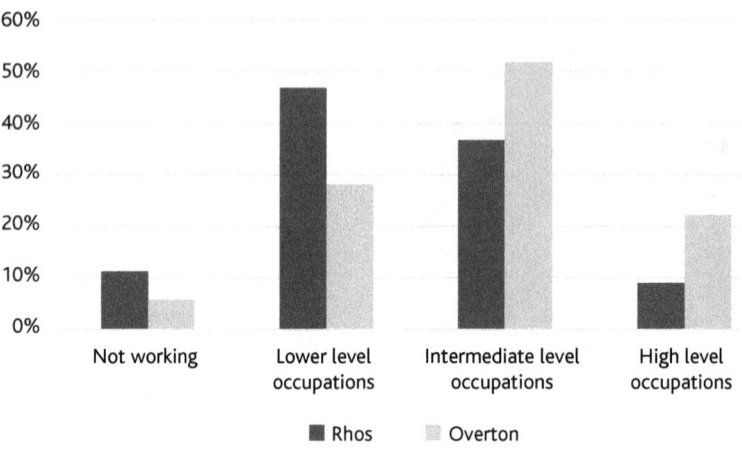

Source: ONS 2011a

for residents. Collating the postcodes in the two villages, the most common categories in Overton are 'retired and empty nesters' and 'owner occupiers in small towns and villages'. In Rhos, the most common category is 'semi-skilled workers in traditional neighbourhoods'.

The Welsh Index of Multiple Deprivation (WIMD) is the Welsh Government's official measure of relative deprivation for small areas in Wales and identifies areas with the highest concentrations of several different types of deprivation (Figure 3.5). WIMD ranks all small areas in Wales from one (most deprived) to 1,909 (least deprived). According to the index, the average ranking for Rhos is 935 which is just below the mean average score for areas in Wales (954), while Overton is ranked 1,493 which places it in the least deprived 20 per cent of areas. On every measure apart from 'access to services', Rhos has higher average deprivation scores than Overton.

An obvious difference between Rhos and Overton linking present-day community to the past is the extent of Welsh language use (Figure 3.6). Rhos' history and position within the Welsh Maelor as opposed to Overton in the English Maelor is reflected in modern statistics on the use of Welsh in everyday life. According to the 2011 Census, in Rhos a quarter of the population speak Welsh with a further 11 per cent having a good understanding of spoken Welsh. In Overton, only 9 per cent speak some Welsh – mostly young people who are mandated to study Welsh in school. The proportion of Welsh-speakers in Rhos across age groups reflects changes in how the language has been observed over nearly a century, from a time in the middle of the last century when being a first-language Welsh speaker was often perceived as a barrier to progress (Laidlaw 1995: 193), to later in

**Figure 3.5:** Wales Index of Multiple Deprivation (deciles), 2019

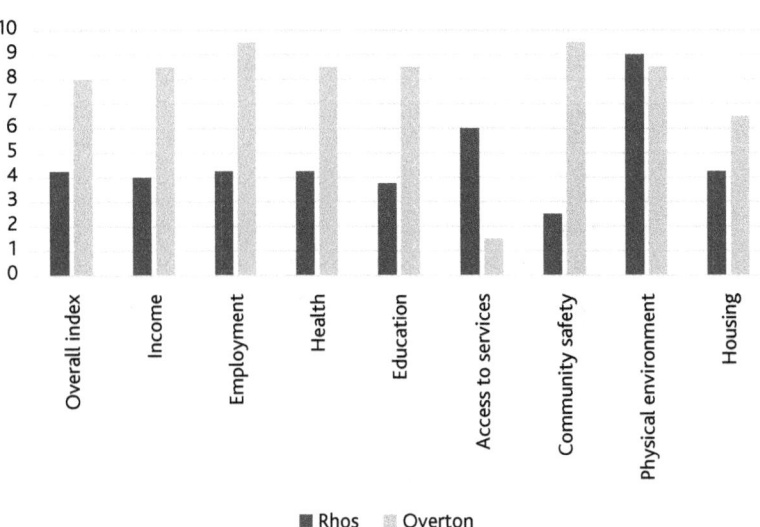

the century when language activists were prominent in Rhos and learning Welsh was eventually made compulsory in schools – the effect of which can be seen in the similar proportion of children speaking Welsh in both villages.

We have therefore, two villages which contrast in both the economic and social profiles of their residents. Yet while Rhos might be viewed as a mainly working-class village, and Overton a predominantly middle-class settlement, Rhos is a fairly typical place in the context of Wales with a not insignificant middle class, while equally in Overton, there are significant numbers of working-class inhabitants. What is interesting for us is how participation and small-scale civil society plays out in each village given the influence not only of social class, but the very different histories and traditions and the extent to which these effect how residents see themselves and feel attached to each place.

## Self-image and perceptions

While official statistics can provide a veneer of understanding as to the kind of local civil society that might be present in each village, literature (for example Dallimore et al 2018) suggests that patterns of involvement are shaped through formations and constructions of identity and belonging. While data relating to these themes was prominent in our ethnographic findings, to obtain a wider picture we carried out a 'street survey' in both villages using semi-structured interviews with residents. These took place in public places including libraries, cafes, along the main streets

**Figure 3.6**: Language spoken

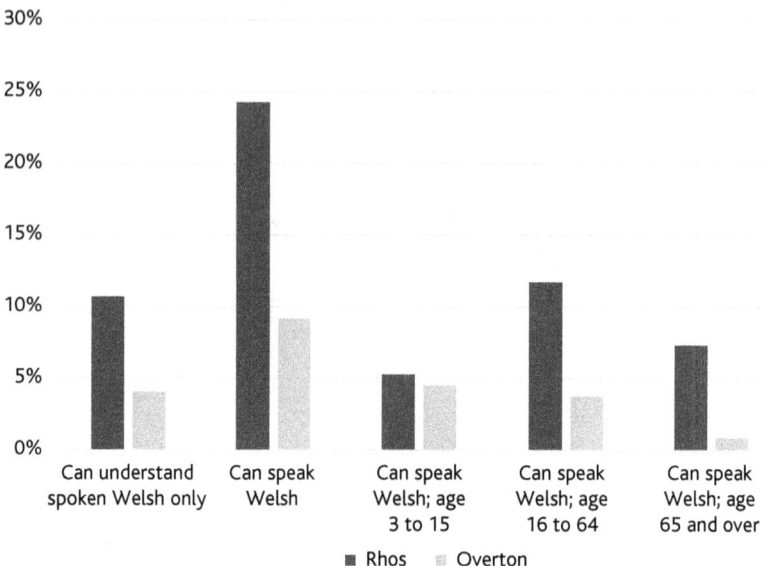

Source: ONS 2011b

and at different local events. We based our survey questions on similar investigations undertaken as part of the National Survey for Wales (Welsh Government 2014) and the Community Life Survey (Cabinet Office 2015) with questions designed to investigate residents' feelings of place identity, belonging and attachment, good and bad things about where people lived, and the extent to which they participated in local associational life. We undertook a small pilot to assess the tool and then with an adapted survey format, we recruited 101 respondents in Rhos and 81 in Overton. We analysed the data from our survey using SPSS software, although with the relatively small samples (C.I.>10) the analysis was restricted to descriptions of frequencies.

To begin exploring the concept of 'place identity' (Lewicka 2008) we asked respondents to tell us how they saw themselves related to a number of geographical scales. As shown in Figure 3.7, responses from the two villages were very different. We found that feelings of identity – any identity – were much stronger in Rhos than Overton. In particular, people in Rhos felt a particular identification with being 'from Rhos' and being Welsh. This may be related to findings from Census data (ONS 2011b) where we observe that 82 per cent of Rhos residents were born in Wales as contrasted with only 52 per cent in Overton. Given other evidence regarding migration patterns, we suspect that of those Welsh-born residents, most were born or brought up in Rhos itself. Residents of Overton had much weaker opinions around their identity in all cases, but particularly

**Figure 3.7**: Notions of place identity (average scores from Likert scale, where 6 is 'feel very strongly' and 1 is 'not at all')

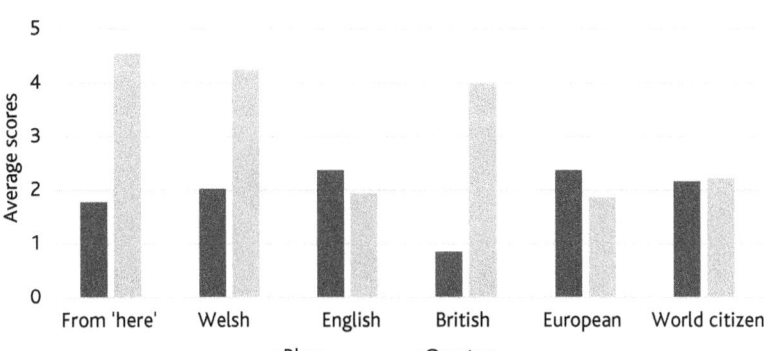

regarding local affiliations. Again, longevity of residence is likely to play a part. In Rhos, nearly 70 per cent of those we interviewed had lived in the village for more than 21 years (52 per cent in Overton), while in Overton, 32 per cent of respondents had moved to the village within the past ten years (12 per cent in Rhos).

Using common responses from our pilot survey as prompts, we asked residents in both villages about what was good, and what was not so good about living in their respective villages. In both cases, a large proportion of residents said that the strong sense of community was important, that people were friendly and that people knowing each other was a good thing. Overton residents were more likely to say that community strength and friendship was important, while 'everyone knowing each other' was most important to people in Rhos. This came through strongly in supporting comments made by Rhos residents:

> 'People here are very special – especially the older community which is very, very strong – goes back to the mines.' (Rhos resident)

> 'Rhos is a close-knit community. There's always someone around to help. Friends and family are all close by.' (Rhos resident)

> 'People have very high standards. We have a special culture here – the Welsh dialect, the Stiwt, Welsh culture particularly.' (Rhos resident)

Figures 3.8 and 3.9 show that, in general Overton residents were more likely to focus on positive aspects of life in their village, while in Rhos, many more people felt that there was little to do and that facilities were poor. Concerns

**Figure 3.8**: What would you say are the best things about living in Rhos/Overton (allowing multiple responses from each respondent)?

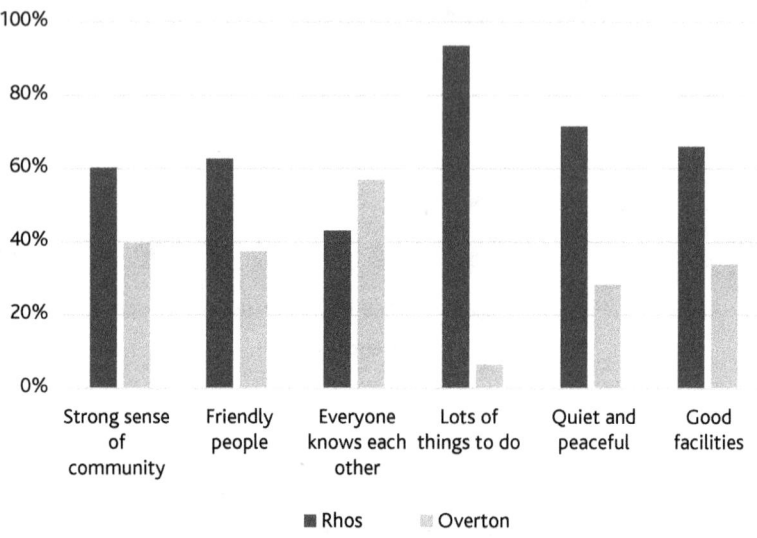

**Figure 3.9**: What would you say are the worst things about living in Rhos/Overton (allowing multiple responses from each respondent)?

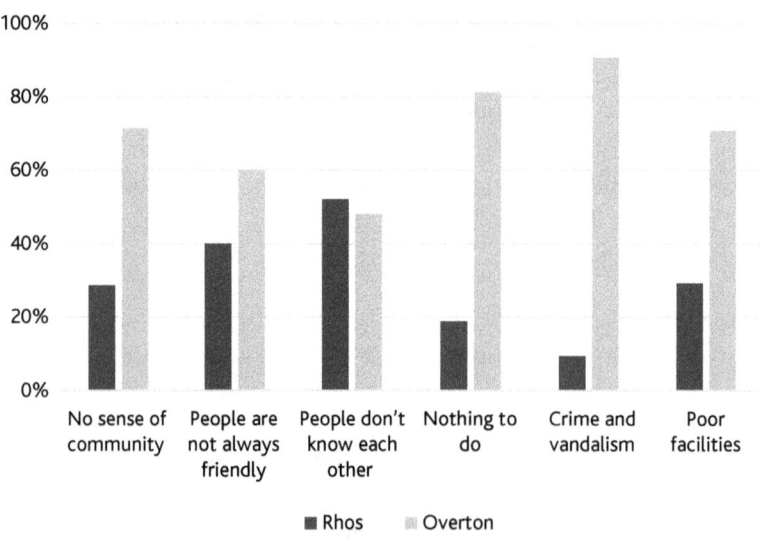

about crime were also high on the agenda of Rhos residents. We heard from many in both villages how change was perceived to be negative, and a threat to individual and collective life:

'It's changed a lot. New people moving here and younger generation don't have the same connection to the place.' (Rhos resident)

'There's not a lot here any more. The Stiwt is all there's left. It's everything. Pubs are closing, so the darts teams have gone. People are becoming more and more insular.' (Rhos resident)

'With increasing population there are more 'strangers', and the community spirit lessens.' (Overton resident)

'Too many people who move into Overton don't know how to live in a village.' (Overton resident)

We asked people to give us an overall indication on a scale of 1 (dissatisfied) to 6 (very satisfied) of how happy they were living in their village. Average scores for residents were not that dissimilar: 5.3 out of 6 in Overton, and 4.6 in Rhos. Findings from similar surveys (National Survey of Wales 2014) might suggest that factors such as rurality and affluence would engender greater life satisfaction in a village like Overton. On the other hand, living in a Welsh-speaking area such as Rhos may also be associated with higher satisfaction than might otherwise be expected.

The Welsh language certainly provides a distinctive characteristic that clearly impacts on village life in a variety of ways. For many Rhos residents that we surveyed, the language was central in village life – something that bound people together and created a rich associational life. Many Rhos residents talked about the 'Welsh culture' of Rhos with the language – and local dialect – at its heart, but also bound up with family and kinship and the traditions of theatre, music and choral singing in particular that was a legacy of the working-class nonconformist past. Yet other Rhos residents – both Welsh and monoglot English speakers – also recognised that the language could be divisive, cutting across class and other boundaries:

'Incomers don't understand the ways of Rhos – we have a way of our own. Chapels, Welsh language, the Stiwt – that kind of thing.' (Rhos resident)

'Some people speak Welsh to exclude others – and I know this as a Welsh speaker. The way that the language is used divides people.' (Rhos resident)

In Overton, language was not an issue. While the census records a small number of Welsh speakers, we came across none in our survey and the local librarian told us that only one resident had ever asked for Welsh language books. Images of the past loomed large in how residents described their relationship with the villages they lived in, and we attempted to capture these views of change by asking whether things had got better or worse over time. One of the weaknesses of our survey is that almost inevitably with an opportunity sample, we interviewed more older than younger people, and there is plenty of evidence that older people are much more likely to hold more negative views about modern life compared with their experience of the past. While this was true in Rhos, in Overton there was an extremely positive view of change with nearly 70 per cent of residents saying that the area had improved over their tenure (Figure 3.10).

Supporting comments suggest that the loss of facilities such as shops, pubs, chapels and leisure opportunities in Rhos was behind much of the negativity. Overton has experienced similar losses, but has managed to maintain a core of services that local residents feel are necessary for a satisfactory life. At the time of our survey, a local bus service was under threat, but with car ownership very high in the village, few residents said that it would directly affect them.

The evidence around identity and belonging in the two areas resonates with findings from many previous village studies. Rhos, like Frankenberg's Pentre (1957), Cohen's Whalsay (1982) or Savage's Ramsbottom (2005) would seem to perpetuate a historic local attachment. While critical of change, many residents were able to retain a sense of moral ownership partly

**Figure 3.10:** Would you say that over the time you have lived in this area it has got better or worse to live in, or would you say things haven't changed much?

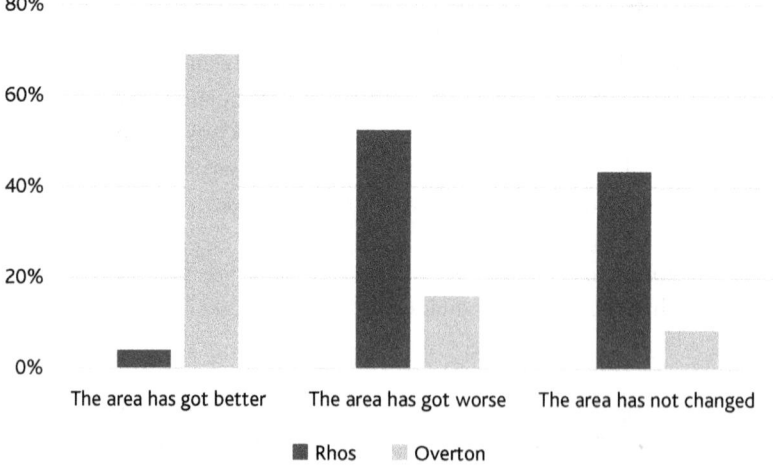

through the use of the Welsh language, the language of class and collective memory of their religious and industrial past. In contrast, in Overton we observe what might be seen as 'elective belonging' (Savage et al 2005: 61) with a solidarity among those who live there that arises not from having historical roots in the place, but from appropriating space and constructing and re-constructing an idealised version of village life (Pahl 2008; Benson and Jackson 2013).

## Local civil society structures

Given the differing profiles of identity and belonging across the two villages, it is not surprising to find very different constructions of local civil society and associative practices. We made an initial assessment of local structures through a combination of desk and fieldwork. Village noticeboards, posters in shop windows, social media sites and word of mouth were all helpful in mapping the range of local organisations and groups in each village. Yet, as the kind of groups we were interested in are mainly small unincorporated associations and consequently 'under the radar' (McCabe et al 2010) and away from official gaze, we cannot be certain that we captured them in their entirety.

Much of the participative activity we observed in Rhos represents an almost clichéd picture of Welsh working-class culture, steeped in industrial, religious and linguistic heritage. The most prominent activity is choral singing and to our knowledge, Rhos has five active choirs. Formed in 1891 the Rhos Male Voice Choir (MVC) is widely recognised as being one of Wales' foremost choirs. It has around 50 members – as well as a youth choir – and performs across the country and regularly tours internationally. As with many working-class cultural institutions, competition is an important part of choral tradition, and Rhos MVC has achieved first prize at the National Eisteddfod of Wales many times, won at the Llangollen International Musical Eisteddfod several times and twice won the BBC Radio Choir of the Year competition – remarkable achievements for a small community. In addition, there is the Rhos Orpheus MVC; a Pensioners' Choir; a Girls' Choir; and the Rhos Singers, a mixed voice choir all active in the village. Until relatively recently, Rhos also had a successful Silver Band and although now renamed Wrexham Brass, it still contains many players from Rhos. Other cultural groups include a youth theatre and the Friends of the Stiwt, a group dedicated to supporting the cultural life of the village through the Miner's Institute. Sporting associations include a rugby club, crown green bowling and pigeon racing. Yet, in other respects for a village the size of Rhos we found few other groups or associations. It would seem that unless an activity has cultural and historical resonance it has little place in local life. The extent to which this configuration of associative life in Rhos has been influenced by migration patterns is an important question, particularly when contrasted with our findings in Overton.

Considering the relatively small population of Overton we found exceptional numbers of associations and groups varying in structure and formality. Unsurprisingly, there were the kinds of associations and groups that one might imagine a quintessential village to have, such as the Women's Institute (although Overton has two competing branches), Cub and Scout groups, British Legion, cricket, football, tennis and bowls clubs, school fete committee, parent and toddler groups, the flower and produce show committee and the school parent and teacher association. Yet in Overton we also found groups that one might more commonly find in larger and more urban communities such as the twinning association – which organises an annual exchange with a village in the French Alps; the amateur dramatic society – which puts on regular performances in the village; a blues, roots and real ale festival group; and the Overton Oracle local newspaper publishing group. We also found a large number of more informal associations where residents came together around an interest, or to tackle a specific issue. These included a walking group, yoga classes, art classes, community choir, medieval music group, litter-picking group and a community gardening group which plants and looks after a number of public spaces in the village. Finally, were a number of voluntary associations or registered charities that facilitated other associative activity such as the Community Council, the Village Hall Management Committee and the Sports & Recreation Club (Figure 3.11).

**Figure 3.11:** Thinking back to when you were growing up, did you participate in any of the following activities?

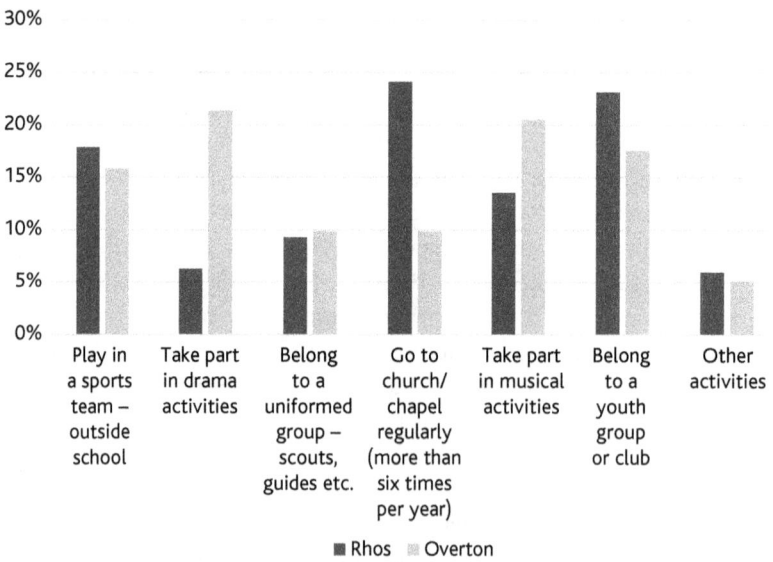

If there is a rural native/urban incomer divide in Overton then the kinds of associational activity we found would seem to be transformative. Perhaps what we see in a village such as Overton is best described by Pahl (1968: 30): 'A village may best be understood as a state of mind. As "rural" people acquire an urban outlook and "urban" people try to escape from the physical urban world into an arcadian vision of a "rural" area.' In other words, the inward migration of middle-class urban escapees into Overton support what they see as traditional rural activities, and through this association bring with them new ideas to enthuse existing residents. Cultural urbanisation would seem to be enhanced by immigration in Overton, creating a greater degree of homogeneity. Benson and Jackson (2013) propose an urban/rural divide in how migrants to an area perform differently in the performativity and processes of place-making. In urban settings they argue that residents focus on 'place-making' to construct place-identity, whereas when moving to rural settings, they focus on 'place-maintenance' to uphold the image of their village as the rural idyll. In Overton, the breadth of association may be the consequence of both place-making and place-maintenance occurring in tandem, while in Rhos, immigration and emigration can be seen to emphasise and build on existing divides allowing little space for change in place identity to occur.

## Local civil society practice

To capture the extent of associative practice in the villages, we asked residents in our street survey to tell us about the ways in which they participate in non-work activities outside the home. Most of those that we spoke to who participated in social activities in both villages, did so in the place, or very near to where they lived.

Patterns of migration mean that responses from Rhos residents were more likely to represent levels of associative activity by young people in Rhos in the past. In Overton, with residents often having grown up in other parts of the country, responses may represent a more generalised picture of past participation.

Responses across the two villages were similar, other than for church-going among Rhos residents, and involvement in drama among people in Overton. Overall, 88 per cent of Rhos residents recalled participating in associative activities when they were younger. In Overton, 96 per cent of residents recalled participating in their youth. Given the age ranges of those taking part in the survey it is difficult to draw firm conclusions from this question. The narratives of Rhos residents have been previously recorded (Laidlaw 1995) as recalling a past where every young person was a member of the Aelwyd,[5] the Band of Hope,[6] or another chapel youth group, yet this may only hold true for residents of a certain age as in many cases those institutions have long ceased to exist.

**Figure 3.12:** Thinking about now, do you participate in any of the following outside the home?

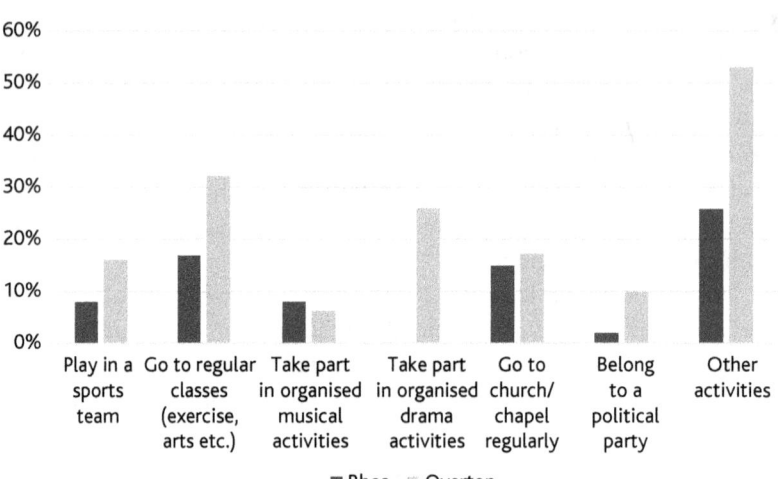

Unsurprisingly, given the number of associations and groups in each village, among adult respondents we see far greater levels and breadth of contemporary participation in Overton than in Rhos. In Overton, 76 per cent of residents interviewed said that they participate in activities outside the home, compared with just 49 per cent in Rhos. Even church or chapel-going is higher in Overton than in Rhos which may be challenging for many residents' construction of place identity (Figure 3.12).

Overall, we found that among the residents we spoke to, just over 50 per cent participated in social activities in Rhos, while in Overton it was 84 per cent. We also observed gender differences with more men than women participating in Rhos, while in Overton, the reverse was true (Figure 3.13).

Finally, we asked residents about other forms of participation including volunteering, campaigning and membership of online groups. Thirty-five per cent of Rhos residents said that they regularly volunteer, compared with 56 per cent in Overton. In both cases, this is higher than the Wales average of 28 per cent (Welsh Government 2017) but differ in the types of volunteering undertaken. In Overton, much of the volunteering is related to the maintenance of community groups with many residents sitting on organising or coordinating committees. Other volunteering in Overton included less formal activities such as keeping the village tidy, organising church flowers, helping at lunch clubs for the elderly, visiting elderly residents or disabled people and helping out local charities. In Rhos, people talked about their volunteering as more personal, involving helping and caring mainly for family, neighbours and friends. A good proportion of residents in both villages were or had recently been involved in campaigning (25 per

**Figure 3.13**: Residents participating by gender

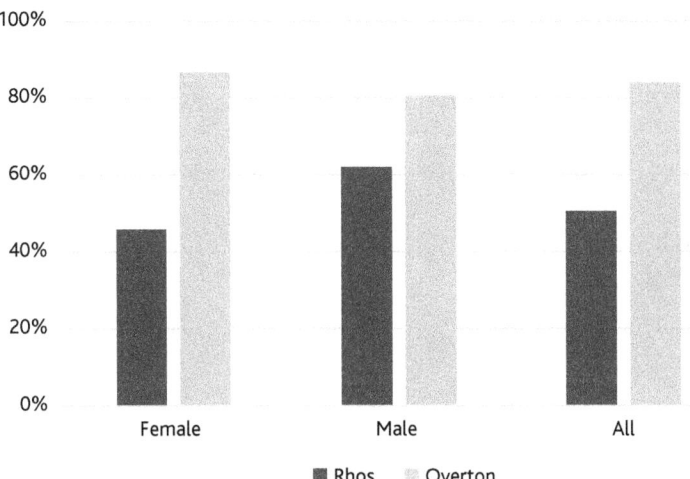

cent in Rhos, 52 per cent in Overton). In both cases, campaigning was around local issues. For example, in Overton, there was opposition to the local council's development plan which set out plans for land around Overton for new housing. In Rhos, the 'Friends of the Stiwt' were continuing a campaign to keep the Miner's Institute open. Few residents in either village talked about belonging, or regularly participating in online groups, although since our research began we have observed an increase in the number of local Facebook groups, so this may be changing. Where online groups have been created in both villages, they reflect existing associations and groups rather than being wholly 'virtual' spaces.

## Conclusion

The focus of our study is in understanding local social relations within theories of civil society. In doing so we examine one of the fundamental social processes: the construction and maintenance of boundaries and identities. In this chapter we have examined evidence which gives some context to how such boundaries and identities might form.

In both villages we observe the enduring importance of morphology and history. It might be argued that contemporary local civil society has its roots in pre-history when geology endowed each landscape with different properties that define the subsequent industrial or agrarian human histories. Alternatively, it could be reasonably claimed that patterns of medieval land ownership retain influence in how each village is bounded and how residents still see themselves today. These factors and others have clearly shaped the ways in which the economies and social structures of each place have developed and explain some of the differences we observe in both official data and our own investigations. We can, therefore, demonstrate how a sense of difference is constructed, and while the places we study may not be fixed and bounded in the ways they once were, we observe how most people's participation remains rooted and locally orientated, challenging the notion that local civil society is inevitably being hollowed out by the global.

# 4

# Civil society through the narratives of place and time

This chapter examines the long-term emotional connections between individual biography and place identity, and their importance for the building and sustaining of local civil society structures over time. To do this we provide a biographical analysis of two individual cases – Ifor (79 at the time of the interview) from Rhos, and Linda (68 at the time of the interview) from Overton, both of whom present us with narrative accounts of their involvement in the production of local newspapers. Through this biographical analysis, we identify the narrative patterns of nostalgia, understood as the 'concern with something which is about to disappear' (Adam 1990: 141), that underpin the organisational structures and actions of local civil societies in both Overton and Rhos. Elements of nostalgia in the biographical narratives point us towards the organisational structures of local civil society, internal power structures, and access to the shared resources that directly, but often informally, underpin the hierarchies of local actors and the opportunities for civil society participation.

We begin by discussing the conceptual relationship between civil society participation and biography. Following this, we outline the narrative framing of the community in the time and space across the two localities. In the second half of the chapter we discuss two types of civil society narratives, based on the notion of solidarities and dialogue, and their impact on the organisation, mission statement and self-governance of those civil society initiatives.

## Narrating civil society

In Chapter 1, we outlined Kaldor's (2003: 585) process-oriented approach to civil society and its relevance for the analysis of individual biographies of participation. As we discussed, Kaldor's (2003) definition of civil society has a particular emphasis on individuals. This is not to say that those individuals cannot be part of the larger groupings or social movements, but by allowing for the conceptualisation of civil society in terms of individual participation, it can capture 'below the radar' activities, often performed over the lifetime, and misleadingly deemed too ordinary to be considered as a key aspect of social change. The biographical aspects of civil society, however, include the processes of reasoning behind the choice to participate or not, the mode of action and the biographical consequences of these choices interwoven into the tapestry of the individual life story. Furthermore, the definition sees civil society as a *process* which resonates well with the biographical aspect of long-term participation, through the life course as well as across generations. It highlights both struggle and cooperation, including biographical periods of hardship and discontent as well as phases of relative wellbeing and prosperity. Finally, the definition sees civil society not in separation from both state and economy, but as a platform of interaction between these two social orders and individual agency. Thus, from the biographical perspective, we can appreciate the importance of economic prosperity for the facilitation of voluntary activities, not only regarding the time that individuals can commit to their actions but also in the availability of physical and material resources, such as space to assemble and funds to manage operations. At the same time, changes in the economic situation of people, such as the decline of an industry, may cause a backlash against both the state and employers in the form of industrial actions or acts of civil disobedience.

The conceptualisation of civil society regarding participation in place and over time resonates well with the biographical narratives, where everyday experiences are embedded in the social ties of local communities, family relations and organisational behaviour. Biographical narratives give us two important insights into the processes of building emotional ties of belonging at the individual level as well as negotiating access to the social structures at the level of community. Firstly, biographical narratives are embedded in the sentimental sense of place, not in terms of descriptions of physical buildings and organisation of the space, but in terms of emotional attachments towards specific localities, and symbolic representations of belonging, based on local knowledge of symbolic boundaries where the aspects of who belongs and who does not are being negotiated (Cohen 1985). Secondly, the biographical narrative brings up a temporal aspect of the participation. Uniquely, it blends both the historical and the individual biographical timeframe, indicating the process of social remembering and building the ties of belonging, based on shared memories of biographical experiences, and the sense of togetherness in time reaching both into the past and the future (Cresswell 2009). Biographical narratives give us 'a multidimensional classification or mapping of the human world and our places in it, as individuals and as members of collectives' (Ashmore et al 2004: 5). It is our argument that through understanding these relationships between individual experiences and social roles within the community we can build our knowledge of how local communities construct and manage their civil society structures, both formal and informal, based on the complex reciprocal interdependence of individual and group.

Biographical narratives and our particular focus on participation in place and over time emphasise the processes of reflexive self-organisation of individuals at the local level. This self-organisation is the critical analytical pathway which combines the individual practices of participation, rooted in the biographical sense of belonging and links them to the structures of local civil society, understood as a sphere of both cooperation and resistance within and against the political and economic social orders. This process of taking action in the broader interest of the community, participation, is embedded in the specific locality, reflects its unique symbolic universe (Berger and Luckmann 1966) and builds on the sense of continuity, that organises and mobilises local structures. It forms the tentative first layer of civil society. To fully illustrate these emotional lenses that shape participation we need to see the place through the eyes of participants and walk the mile in their own 'biographical' shoes to recognise the symbolic landscape and informal social hierarchies that are an organic base for civil society participation.

## Symbolic universes of everyday life

Narratives of place, especially those based on the biographical accounts, present a unique source of data. Rather than focusing on exact factual descriptions of physical or geographical spaces, they provide a 'mental mapping' (Lynch 1960; 1972) of the space, highlighting the symbolic boundaries between 'us' and 'them', unique identity symbols and perceptions of the place, as seen through the eyes of people with lifelong emotional and social attachments. This perspective on the place, which is often portrayed as overly subjective and unreliable, we see as a foundation for individual and collective actions which constitute the organic matter of local civil society. In our fieldwork, we focused on the two localities, Rhos and Overton, geographically close, but sociologically very different. The discussion of those two cases illustrates the significance of the symbolic landscape of place, with its unique sense of history and culture, language and geography. It is marked by a number of symbolic boundaries, some highly visible, others quite unconscious and unreflective. Those are reproduced in the structures of local civil society, and reflect a local distribution of social and political power as well as official and unofficial hierarchies directly influencing participation in the local community, with respect to everyday engagement and leadership.

Our selection of two biographical cases illustrates the contrast between different perceptions of civil society participation. To enhance the contrast between the places we selected, we chose two narrators who hold similar positions within each locality. Both edit village newspapers. In both cases the local press is one of the central focal points for civil society participation and activities. The localities under investigation each have their press representative: *Nene* in Rhos and the *Overton Oracle*. These publications are committed to serving their respective villages and form a significant part of local civil society. They are written and edited by the local community. They aim to inform and organise local activities as well as cultivate the sense of belonging and local pride. They are pillars of local civil society. Although a lot can be said about these two places from the analysis of the content of the papers, this is not what this particular study is aiming to achieve. Instead, we interviewed the people at the helm of these papers to learn through their biography how they committed to the mission of editing a local paper and how their perception of the place they live in, including the complexity of its social relations, is represented in the organisational structures of the editorial teams and the mission statements of the papers. The two cases are outlined in the following section.

## Case 1: Ifor and the case of *Nene*

Ifor comes from an established Rhos family. He was brought up in the village by his mother and grandparents. He attended an all-boys local grammar school and continued his education at Aberystwyth university, studying Latin, English and Welsh. After university, he was appointed a teacher of English and Welsh in a number of schools around Rhos. His career, as well as his personal goals, concentrate on the revitalisation of the Welsh language in the community. He is very engaged in the action of bringing Welsh media to the village, opening the Welsh-medium school and nursery and celebrating the uniqueness of Rhos' Welsh dialect. The idea of preserving and celebrating Welsh in the village was a driving force for establishing a local newspaper, known in Welsh as a '*papur bro*', covering the community issues of Rhos. *Nene* was founded in 1977 and its name is drawn from the local and unique Welsh dialect (meaning 'that' and pronounced 'nai nai'). Ifor mentions that 30 people were involved at the beginning and the first issues were paid for from donations. Today the editorial team is quite small and consists of the people who over time were the most reliable. Today *Nene*'s financial existence depends on grants received from the Welsh Language Board. Distribution is through the local shops and postal delivery. Sales have varied over the years from 1,000 copies to around 650 nowadays. The readership is mostly local, but some copies are shipped worldwide to America and New Zealand. The paper does not have an online presence. The newspaper is around 20 pages, printed in colour. *Nene* is produced exclusively in Welsh and prioritises local issues – news, chapel commentaries, school announcements, the local economy and also contains fierce editorials. Ifor summarises a mission statement of *Nene* as 'a protector of community life'. He says, "Anything that would endanger the social life of Rhos, and especially the Welsh life, we would raise the banner."

## Rhos through the eyes of Ifor

Rhos is a place with a very clearly defined identity, proud of its mining history and Welsh working-class culture. The mining heritage is visible not only in the architecture of the places such as the Stiwt but also at the level of language. The uniqueness of Rhos in Ifor's biographical narrative lies in its single-minded focus on the language. Not merely the Welsh language, but a distinctive Rhos dialect. In his narrative, this aspect of social life is a symbol of Rhos' unique history and identity. It is via Rhos' particular words and expressions that Ifor maps out the symbolic landscape of his home village. Focusing on just two words from his narrative '*beindin*' and '*nene*' gives an insight into identity structures of the place.

The first word Ifor mentions in his narrative is '*beindin*', which in Rhos dialect means 'that little bit extra'. '*Beindin*' comes from the coal mines and designates the leftover part of rock, which was preserved to secure the roof, but the word is used throughout Ifor's narrative to illustrate the attitude of generosity and readiness of the people of Rhos to give something extra to the community. In the text, discussing the finances of *Nene*, Ifor says:

> 'But we're lucky in Rhos, the level of subscription is excellent. The idea of everyone in Rhos supporting each other – that's very strong. And people are very generous. The ones who buy yearly subscriptions, they always give anything they have left over. They call that *beindin* … So it always pays for the paper, which is around ten pounds for the yearly subscription, and then the *beindin* of around 15 pounds on top of that. We're lucky to have that.'

The use of the word designates the cultural and ethnographic imprint the coal mining industry left in the identity of Rhos. As a mining community, Rhos was a place of hard-working men, who after the day spent on the physical work lived their life between a chapel and a pub. Mining was not just a job; it shaped the way the village lived. '*Beindin*' is a direct metaphor taken from the mines and transplanted into the identity of the place. It seems to say people of Rhos are hard-working folks, but they are also generous and share their wealth for the wellbeing of all. The symbolic boundary here is class-related: hard work is a value, so too is contributing to the wellbeing of others. However, '*beindin*' evokes the tones of nostalgic narrative (Blokland 2001; Bennett 2018). After all, Rhos is not a mining village anymore. The use of the 'past' as a symbolic category which aims to elicit specific memories shows how Ifor creates the distinction between 'us' who remember the glorious past, and 'others' who do not. He places himself and others like him in 'an explicit moral relationship with the past community' (Bennett 2018: 5).

This relationship is additionally reinforced by the linguistic diversity of Rhos. The use of Rhos' unique dialect is meant to draw yet another symbolic boundary between those native to Rhos and the newcomers and outsiders. Even the title of the paper *Nene* is written in Rhos' Welsh and its main mission is the preservation of this linguistic heritage. When asked about the origin of the paper's name Ifor recalls the following story:

> 'And there was an element of teasing going on, with the result that Rhos children were afraid of using their language ... Schoolchildren from Bod Hyfryd in Wrexham used to make fun of school children in Rhos for saying *nene* and *ene*. ... the meaning of *nene*, it's used in Rhos more than anywhere else as far as I know, and so that gives it meaning, at least for people from around here. It means *hwnna yne* 'that one there'. ... So, *Nene*. But that's the background of choosing the name. It either reflects a particular place in the area, or something special about the society, or the language. And it was the language for us, hence *Nene*.'

The phrase 'language for us' is rooted in the conviction that Rhos' Welsh is under threat, not only by the decline in usage but also by other forces, such as teasing the school children for speaking Rhos. Its use is aimed to straighten the perception of 'us' versus 'them' and provide a moral justification – such as saving a language – for excluding certain groups within Rhos from the shared experience of writing and reading *Nene*. The consequences of this type of moral judgement based on the protection of the language becomes so embedded within the 'identity' of the paper that when asked for information about the local 'community café' initiative, *Nene*'s editors refused to interview the owner who is an outsider to Rhos, with the justification that "I have a feeling that they aren't Welsh speakers".

This landscape of symbolic boundaries directly affects the readership of the *Nene*, and the selection of topics covered, but also has a powerful impact on the structure of the editorial board. To be a part of *Nene* is to be a part of a tight and weathered group of people who set the tone for the public debates and reinforce the symbolic boundaries of the community. Ifor is one of the two key people involved in the process of writing, editing, publishing and distribution of the paper. The editorial board is very much the same as it has been for the last 37 years. Some people from the inner circle have died and have not been replaced, others come and go, but the group itself is very exclusive:

> 'Some people would come in and join us, but it was an intermittent thing for obvious reasons. But no, that would happen within the setting circle, in *Nene*'s circle. So the setting thing was never, well, it wasn't

something that belonged to the wider society. Anybody was welcome to come in and see us if they wanted, but nobody bothered. They were happy enough to get the paper.'

*Nene*'s exclusivity carries all the landmarks of the clique. The group prides itself on a work ethic represented by the timely distribution of the paper (11 issues a year) and 37 years of public service for Rhos' community and at the same time excludes all other contributors as relatively unreliable, including even the input from local Welsh schools. Ifor claims that the editorial team structure assures the quality and continuity of the paper in providing a valuable public service, but this is to the point of sacrificing any innovation and novelty, a new inflow of ideas and the access to participation for any other Rhos-born or Rhos-raised, or non-Rhos individuals.

This raises the issue of the continuity of the paper. In his narrative, Ifor says: "We're not getting any younger. So, if anything happened to either anyone of us – that would instantly mean the end of the paper." This type of finality in the narrative seems to have two main points. On the one hand in Ifor's perception, the editorial board and his involvement in the paper are the same as the existence of the paper. And on the other hand, it adds the feel of finality to the project of *Nene* as well as 'old Rhos'.

## Case 2: Linda and the case of the *Overton Oracle*

Linda moved to Overton as a young adult with husband and children for her husband's employment. In 1967 they bought a house in Overton. Linda focused on raising a young family. As a daughter of a teacher and engineer, Linda mentions that education was always an essential part of her upbringing. After college she became a teacher herself, but after her children were born, she focused on their upbringing. Linda has been actively engaged in the community from the beginning, she was involved in setting up the playgroup in Overton and then got engaged in the Wrexham and Clwyd committees for the Pre-school Playgroup Association. Once her children had grown up, she decided to give up the playgroup activities and got a job as an Education Officer at the local National Trust. She retired in 2011. Her husband James worked for a company that relocated a number of times, forcing him to travel to work. At the age of 50 he was made redundant, started his own company, but in 2002 joined the National Trust as a manager and retired at the age of 61.

Linda and her husband are joint-editors of *Overton Oracle*. She recalls that the newspaper started in 1999, as an extension to the existing biannual community newsletter. For the first couple of years, they had an official editor, but after he left the paper unexpectedly, she and her husband found themselves holding that position for the last ten years. The editorial board is a tight-knit group, but it involves both newcomers and old citizens of Overton. The newspaper is financially self-sufficient, with the income from advertising and some community council grants. It is distributed monthly, door-to-door by volunteers for free to the whole village and has a robust online presence (all recent issues are available online). The *Overton Oracle* is usually eight pages long, with contributions from the community, such as chapels and schools. The aim is to keep people informed and engaged in active community life.

## Overton from Linda's perspective

In contrast to Rhos, Overton's place identity is centred around the idea of the estate village. It means that it has been founded on estate land, owned through generations by one particular family. This family controlled the property development and took patronage over the community's focal points, such as the church and community centre. Due to that paternalistic relationship with the estate, the village avoided development expansion and kept its idealised and highly valued village charm. Overton fits well with the representation of the 'village in mind' (Pahl 2005). The idea of a country living that over the years has attracted many middle-class incomers, particularly from England, who searched for a quiet place to live and vibrant community. This middle-class idea of the village life has its symbolic landmarks, such as a well-established pub, shops, library, village hall and the church.

According to Linda, the most significant part of the symbolic landscape of Overton is the person, an embodiment of its proud history and the heir of the family who owned the estate, nicknamed by the village 'The Squire'. He is an 80-year-old gentlemen who 'is still a father figure of the village', and has 'this patriarchal thing going on, almost the lord of the manor'. The Squire is a symbolic link between the Overton village now and the past. His presence gives locals a sense of historical continuity of the stately manor and makes them feel like they share and co-create this element of Overton's heritage. Linda described The Squire in the following manner:

> 'Although, if you meet him, he will be mowing the lawns. He is a scruffy old man who mows the lawn in the churchyard. Because he rarely turns up at church and he says, "This is when I meet my God". In a filthy pair of old trousers and he mows the lawn. It saves them employing a gardener. So, he is the nicest bloke.'

His presence seems very unobtrusive, up to the point that some people do not know who he is and what his role is in the community. However, for those like Linda and James, he is the one with the power to *invite* incomers into well-established community structures. When discussing the beginnings of their involvement with the local newspaper the couple tell the story of the Friends of St Mary's Church:

> 'He started this little group called Friends of St Mary's. He was very concerned that the church goes from hand to mouth and that, if anything happened, like a big hole in the roof or whatever, there was no fund. ... And so he wanted to set up a fund just for the fabric of the historic building, and I think we were both invited because we both worked for the National Trust at the time. ... He was very clever, yes, two people are old villagers, and there are two of us who are new villagers. But yes, that was a very nice mixture, so that he got both sides of the village. And you very much got a flavour of the old village from this couple.'

This group of people forms the core of an informal power structure within the community. It managed to bring together people of Old Overton and newcomers in a way that complemented each other. The Old Overton individuals come with the knowledge of who is who in the community and the newcomers brought in energy and expertise to participate and contribute to the community. This pattern was successfully replicated in a number of other civil society initiatives, including setting up a local paper. The original editorial board was a part of St Mary's group and carried on with the same old Overton and new Overton formula:

> 'Again we've only got a tiny committee, but that's quite good, because we've got two old villagers, who know all the gossip, and especially one of them looks at births, marriages and deaths, because she knows everybody ... And we've got one chap who's our Treasurer, who's fairly new to the village, but he runs the business, so he does the accounts for us. And the rest are incomers.'

The group responsible for the *Overton Oracle* paper is relatively small and over time the people who persisted and overcame trying situations became synonymous with the wellbeing of the newspaper. Due to their age, they face the challenge of the continuity of the paper. They have noticed the lack of the interest among young people. However, differently from Rhos, they seem to be optimistic about the future. They mentioned situations in the past where the future of the paper seemed under threat and where the community came through. They recall:

> 'Financially we are sustainable; it breaks even, more or less. I do worry if I decide to give up, who is in the village, who's prepared to do the time and the skills. But that was what [the past] clerk said ... and we

found somebody. So, I think it's, as we used to say ... it's not until you don't turn up that you find who will take over.'

## Nostalgic narratives of the place and the organisation of civil social actions

Both Rhos and Overton narratives focus on participation as service to the community and local civil society. They re-tell the story of a struggle as well as cooperation with the political and economic circumstances, such as *Nene*'s mission to save Rhos' unique language, but also show how they can use resources and networks to improve people's experiences of living in the village. The narratives discussed earlier show that the form that people choose to tell a story about the place they live in reflects the wider 'mental space' (Schütze and Schröder-Wildhagen 2012), whereby the individuals position themselves within given social networks. Their roles reproduce the existing organisational structures and help direct the mechanisms of self-governance and mobilisation at the community level (Jessop 2020). The narrative of the place, that illustrates the biographical links entwined in the story of place, showcases internal hierarchies and distribution of power and can powerfully include or exclude people who wish to belong. This network of social relations is framed in the narratives of nostalgia and reflects organisation of the local civil society initiatives that underpin the two different modus operandi of local civil society, one embedded in the nostalgic narratives of solidarity, illustrated by Rhos, and the other in the nostalgic narrative of dialogue and civility, illustrated by Overton.

## Civil society in the narrative of nostalgia

The narratives of civil society participation, illustrated by both cases of Rhos and Overton, are embedded in a nostalgic narrative. This type of narrative is an attempt to reconcile the continuity of the individual life within the community, that blends the past, present and the future. In many ways the nostalgic narratives are about the survival of the 'way of life', seeking to capture and preserve the past, such as in the case of Ifor. Nostalgic narratives, however, can also be represented in terms of 'affection towards past' that creates momentum towards the future. Visible in the case of Linda, the preoccupation with continuity is reflected in the issues of succession of the values and civic norms to the future generations. For the analysis of civil society as a field of social action, exploration of nostalgic narratives adds towards our understanding of processes of social mobilisation and their governing principles. The analysis of nostalgic narratives indicates the direction in the perception of temporal continuities, towards the future or the past, that emphasise specific symbolic and moral aspects that are used to mobilise local communities into civil society actions.

## Preserving the past: the case of Rhos

The nostalgic narrative of Rhos, as illustrated by Ifor's biographical narrative, aims to preserve the past. This type of nostalgic narrative would fit Rhos into Barrett's category of those homogeneous communities that 'have one coherent, dominant source of collective identity. Typically, this is place based' (Barrett 2015; see also Wallman 1984; Day 2006b). Such communities are 'likely to invoke backward-looking symbols that build upon a sense of nostalgia for lost traditions' (Barrett 2015: 192). These symbols would be presented as positive, showing the notions of a glorious or at least praiseworthy past, and enhance the perception that their value is lost on the community that we see today.

In his narrative Ifor says: "One hopes that there is still some in the 'Welsh life'. But between my house and the place where we practice [choir practice], you don't hear a word of Welsh. The place is almost foreign in its Englishness, regarding the younger population."

This type of nostalgic narrative, understood as an act of 'selectively remembering the past in the way that supports a negative evaluation of the present situation and displays the past positively as a coherent, comprehensible era' (Blokland 2001: 272). It highlights a powerful symbolic boundary that defines belonging and frames it in the language of solidarities and sacrifice (Jessop 2020) towards a 'lost cause', in this case a notion of 'Welsh life', anchored in memory of the old Rhos. This type of narrative forces the organisational structure of local civil society to prove over and over its commitment to the cause. This cause is represented in the mission statement of *Nene* as the protection of 'Welsh life', including Rhos' unique dialect but also mining, working-class heritage. This type of narrative strictly defines who is a part of Rhos and who is not. In the case of *Nene*, the readers of the paper are Rhos-born and Rhos-Welsh-speaking individuals, who may, but do not necessarily have to, live in Rhos. *Nene* ships internationally to people who follow its nostalgic narrative, even though they may not have lived in Rhos for a long time, but excludes people who actually live in Rhos but do not conform to the necessary requirements of descent and language.

Furthermore, the nostalgic narrative uses the language of personal sacrifice to the cause. For Ifor, running the paper on limited resources and limited staff is a testimony to his commitment. In many respects, even the vision of the paper's decline, after Ifor's death, writes itself into the narrative framework of decline and discontinuity of what is considered noble and pure in the traditions of the past ways of life. This language of personal sacrifice also signals compelling justification for the exclusive role Ifor plays in the newspaper as well as the wider community. He is willing to commit time and resources towards the cause, and this gives him a moral power to judge the who and how of participation and belonging according to this particular vision of Rhos.

## Securing continuity for the future: the case of Overton

The case of Overton presents a future-focused nostalgic narrative, which fits the description of the heterogeneous community (Barrett 2014: 193) that invents new symbols to bring people together, 'build bridges between disparate segments of the community' and appear more forward-looking. In-migration to established neighbourhoods or villages and new multicultural communities exemplify heterogeneous communities, which tend to be inclusive and pluralistic in nature, rather than exclusive.

Overton is a village that anchors its historical sense of continuity, such as the father figure of 'The Squire', to create the sense of authenticity (Bennett 2018: 453) and the type of inclusive identification that can be extended towards the people who wish to participate, rather than for people who are simply destined to be a part of the village. This type of narrative creates the 'idea' of the village life, embedded in the sense of community and cooperation. When asked about the reasons to move to Overton, Linda mentions: "We both came from, we both lived in a village. And so, and I particularly wanted to recreate that life I'd had … the freedom of the fields of the woods and the hills. And I wanted that again."

This sense of nostalgia is not place specific, and the idea of 'fields of the wood and the hills' can be re-created in different locations by the effort and commitment of the individual to the specific place. Here Savage et al's notion of 'elective belonging' finds its ultimate fulfilment (Savage et al 2005). The nostalgia narrative is encouraging for individual participation in village life by allowing multiple entry points into its civil society organisational structures. The inclusive nature of this type of narrative is designed to use the skills and commitment of the individuals for the specific village-based cause. It also allows for the specialisation of the roles according to individual strengths and interests. Linda mentions in her narrative interview the process that all newcomers went through before they were included in the social and cultural life of the village:

> 'And all of us were incomers … and then gradually we all have separate interests, and we all got involved in different things and different elements of the village. And I think that is one of the best things that the village offers, is this opportunity; you can be a bell ringer, you can become a councillor, you can play bowls, you can join the Scouts,

you can join mother and toddler ... But I think, because there have been incomers as well, I think it's often the incomers who've got the energy to do these things.'

The 'energy' and 'new ideas' are the strength of this type of narrative. The *Overton Oracle* as a newspaper has a modern look, colourful print and is available online for everyone to access. It advertises local businesses and is the platform for social mobilisation, where the latest social initiatives, such as the Beer Festival, are being discussed and organised. This type of civil society platform corresponds to Jessop's mode of self-governance (2020) based on dialogue, operating in the reflexive and procedural organisational rationality and taking the shape of the open network. This procedural character of the participation is visible in the relaxed way in which Linda and James are talking about someone else taking over the newspaper. Their understanding is that if they cannot do it, someone else will get a chance to stand up even if they decide to lead the newspaper in a different direction.

## Nostalgic narratives and implications for civil society actions

In both cases nostalgic narratives are directly related to the organisational structures – they indicate the symbolic boundaries, points of access, internal hierarchies, moral justifications and reasoning. They operate on a feedback loop with each narrative reinforcing organisation and vice versa. It is this feedback loop that contributes to the reproduction of the organisational patterns of civil society in the specific place via intrinsic identity discourse that brings the biographical sense of belonging and emotional attachments to place in the unique social environment that nurtures the civil society participation.

The complex nature of this process has three significant consequences for the introduction of social policy and social interventions into the civil society organisations at the local levels. First, it is difficult to change the organisational structure of the local civil society organisation from the outside without running the risk of its collapse. Intervention into the mode of participation, for example including unknown volunteers or paid staff, or the requirement of extensive consultation as the way to receive funding, often interferes with the identity of particular organisation. The key here is the fact that people who participate do it as a part of their biographical identity project, and this type of interference would question and disrupt this type of connection. The outcome would be either the 'cosmetic' type of change aimed to receive the resources or the withdrawal from the organisational structures contributing to its collapse.

Second, the way to introduce effective change is to create the opportunity that can be picked up by the organisation and become a part of a biographical project of the participants. In many respects, it needs to fit the overall narrative of the place and its identity. In case of Rhos, the most successful civil society mobilisation and organisation was around the issue of saving the Stiwt (see Chapter 3) – the Miner's Institute, as a symbol of Rhos' identity as well as the heritage funding for the closed mines. For a place like Overton, on the other hand, the initiatives that support the 'village life' idea – health, wellbeing, environmental activities as well as their pub and church – are the most suitable and the most likely to succeed.

Third, understanding the organisation and identity of the place is not enough without recognition that local civil society organisations should be self-governed. Through the process of participation and commitment of significant part of the biography, the individuals feel ownership over the issues and resources. This sense of ownership is the best guarantee of a community's self-governance. It is when other institutions interfere, either with setting new political agendas, or changing the economic balance of the organisation, that this intrinsic quality of civil society organisation is at risk. By disrupting the link between the identity of the place and people's biographical commitment to it, the state, as well as the economy, can squander the effort and spirit within the local civil society organisations.

## Conclusion

This chapter uses two biographical cases to illustrate the dynamic relationship between the biographical process of shaping belonging and the identity of the place that underpin participation in local civil society. This study outlines two types of nostalgic narratives: *backward-looking*, represented by the village of Rhos, and *forward-looking*, represented by the village of Overton. Those narratives, built upon the emotional connections to the place as well as its particular symbolic landscape and cultural boundaries, directly reflect the organisation and self-governance of the local civil society structures. It is possible to draw the link between the nostalgic type of narrative and the civil society structure based on the notion of solidarity, loyalty and love towards the specific place, and even specific time of the place. At the same time, it is apparent that the nostalgic narrative is also reflected in civil society organisations that use dialogue and procedural logic of operating as an inclusive system, for new people as well as new ideas. This process shows that local civil society requires the foundation of biographical commitment. People who participate need to incorporate the civil society-related social role into their own identity and feel ownership towards the agenda and organisation. This process is very personal and threads a very precarious balance between transparency of the social organisation, highlighting internal hierarchies, and modes of operation, including the process of social inclusion as well as exclusion. Those personal and social relations are built across the lifetime of the individuals and create the first tentative layer of civil society at the local level.

# 5

# Civil society and local associational life

Local associations are a key vehicle for participation in civil society. They operate at a distance from the state, the market and families, with varying degrees of independence and dependence. They are sites of social action, expressing both solidarity and contestation. They bring groups of people together around common interests and shared activities. They may also articulate conflicts and issues of debate. Many are visible in terms of their organisation, membership and outcomes. Others are less visible, more loosely organised, or exist 'below the radar' (McCabe et al 2010). Associations are characterised by a diverse range of actors, repertoires and agendas. At the local level, they have a close identification with place, they depend largely on local social ties and operate mainly within the limits of local space. They are an important constitutive element in most understandings of civil society and its local expressions. But the boundaries between civil society, the state and market are not easy to draw. There are ebbs and flows in the voluntary and statutory sectors as funding fluctuates, partnerships form and dissolve, and as the contexts for voluntary action change. Lewis (1999: 268) concludes that the boundaries between state and civil society became increasingly blurred in the 1990s. In a parallel process, some voluntary associations have had to become more competitive, market-driven and business-like (Han 2017). As discussed in Chapter 1, conceptual debates about state dominance or marketisation of the third sector tend to prioritise the framework of the national state, and scales well above the local.

The impact of these processes below the level of local authorities is relatively under-researched. This chapter uses evidence from our research on the localities of Rhos and Overton to explore these themes in the local 'field of action' of each village. It describes the existing patterns of association in each locality and uses the data to inform debates about civil society theory, including the impact of funding and resources of social capital, the persistence and decline of social networks, the obstacles to participation, and the sources of variation between localities. Our strategy of comparing two localities within the same local authority area is designed to highlight the differences that exist within a shared administrative, political and cultural context – and to explain why they occur.

The chief officer of the county Voluntary Council, which promotes volunteering and social enterprise in the Wrexham area, is well placed to understand the variety and distribution of different types of association. He comments that patterns of participation are shaped by long-term trends: "over the last twenty years [associations] have grown up with lots of local authority funding, which have then made them very reliant on local authorities". However, faced with increasing austerity, the authorities attempt to retain services themselves, rather than externalise or outsource them to the third sector. This creates tension and less local authority-commissioned activity for the third sector. He compares the sector to a three-tier sandwich. The lowest level consists of community-based organisations that are not grant dependent (although they may be grant recipients) and provide services for local benefit. The top level consists of national NGOs like Barnardo's or NSPCC, or international NGOs like the Red Cross, which have expanded significantly and receive income through grants and contracts from government and other statutory sources, as well as private donations. In between is a middle band of associations which fluctuates according to the supply of funding from local authority, National Lottery and other sources – as well as the demand for services. This is an area of relative fluidity, shaped by forces which lead organisations to downsize or forge alliances with larger entities. At the level of scale of our research sites in Rhos and Overton, examples of independent or grant-supported community associations exist alongside middle-tier organisations, while some volunteering takes place with 'top level' bodies that are based outside the localities.

## The question of associations

There is a consensus that the typical features of non-profit, or third sector, associations include voluntary (rather than legally required) membership, a joint purpose which is defined by the association itself through dialogue and negotiation, and at least an element of funding from voluntary contributions (Edwards 2014: 20). Associations take the form of charities, societies, clubs, self-help groups, independent media and social movements. Some have a closer relationship to the market (social enterprises), while others are more strongly linked to the state (through government grant funding, for example).

The extensive literature on local associational life (introduced in Chapter 2) raises questions about its rise and decline, how it is shaped in local contexts and how it relates to the state and market. Putnam (2000) famously provoked a wide debate as to whether participation levels are in decline in Western societies. While in the UK context the case for an overall decline is not proven, there is good evidence that participation in civil society has become increasingly stratified along lines of class and other axes of inequality (Grenier and Wright 2006). The focus of our own questions is on the range and depth of participation in local associations; their sustainability in terms of organisation and funding; and how changes in associational forms and the experiences of local civil society participants are shaped by local contexts. Our comparative research gives us leverage to prise apart such questions, to capture both continuity and change in participation, and to assess the importance of place in understanding local associations.

Our approach was to undertake an initial mapping exercise to establish the main parameters of local associational life, creating a description of the sites of participation, the actors involved, their organisations and the ways in which their associative activity interfaces with the wider world in terms of governance and funding. This was followed up with data from the survey, ethnography and biographical interviews (see details in Chapter 4). The breadth of data allows us to analyse associations as formal organisations, but also investigate motivations, belonging and people's emotional attachments to place – which are likely to change over time and be governed by quite local and situational factors.

## Associations in Rhos

As described previously in Chapter 3, Rhos is a large village with a long industrial tradition, which has experienced significant de-industrialisation in the last 50 years. The pattern of associational life is closely linked to the industrial past, its prominence as a centre of nonconformist religion and its Welsh-speaking identity. Each strand contributes to the tapestry of associations and has strong links to the predominantly working-class traditions of the area. Firstly, there are the associations directly connected to the former mining and extractive industries: the miners' institutes, the trade unions, the recreational associations such as the bowling club, the male voice choirs, and – today – the heritage organisations which promote education and understanding of the industrial past. Secondly, the village was an important centre of the 1904–05 nonconformist religious revival, and chapel-going prospered until the 1950s. The legacy can be seen in the large number of chapel buildings and in the sense of a community identity built on mining and nonconformity. Only some of the chapels remain as centres of worship (Davis et al, 2021) but those which do, function both to maintain services for their members, and as sites for collective participation in social as well as religious activities. Thirdly, the Welsh language, spoken by a significant minority of the village population, is a signifier of the distinctiveness of Rhos in its wider surroundings, despite the evidence of declining use of Welsh among the younger generations. The following sections explore examples of associations from each of these three strands, namely the bowling club, a religious group and the local Welsh medium community newspaper. The role of meeting places is also considered.

*Bowling in Rhos*

The Crown Green bowling green in Rhos is situated in Ponciau Banks Park, an 'urban' park of about seven hectares owned by Wrexham County Borough Council. It is centrally located in the village and overlooked on one side by houses and the Stiwt, and open views to the surrounding countryside of the Dee valley on the other. The park area was reopened after extensive refurbishment in June 2009, funded by the Heritage Lottery Fund (HLF). It includes tennis and basketball courts, a skate park, BMX track, children's play area, bandstand, stone circle and landscape areas of grass and trees. The stone circle commemorates the Park being used as an Eisteddfod site in 1945.

The park hillside remains vivid in local memory for being the place in the 1926 miners' strike where miners dug for coal in small bell-pits for their own fuel. Subsequently, the Miner's Institute Committee and volunteers from the local community worked to turn the derelict Banks into a park, with help from teams of students across Europe from the International Voluntary Service for Peace (Best and Pike 1948), who volunteered at Ponciau in 1932, 1933 and 1935. It was the second such project in Wales, building on the experience of international volunteering at Brynmawr, Gwent. On a visit in 1934, Megan Lloyd George, the first female MP elected in Wales, declared: 'I tour the Ponciau Banks and what do I see? I see here the League of Nations ideal at work. Not destruction, but creation. Not ruin, but planned construction. Not chaos, but beauty. Not a wilderness, but a garden which blossomed as the Rose' (cited in Ellis and Bolton 2016: 59). This green symbol of hope in the depression is now celebrated with commentary and historical photos on one of the prominent display boards in the park.

Today, the Park is staffed by a Park Ranger (one of the interviewees in the study), who is an employee of Wrexham Council with a background in the local area and experience in a number of other parks. This person's job is to assist in the operation, maintenance, security and development of the Park and its associated facilities. The Ranger has a role in applying for grants for a range of activities and is responsible for coordinating events and activities within the park, including environmental education, producing interpretative displays and developing learning materials. There is also a gardener. A local independent group, the 'Friends of Ponciau Banks', supports the maintenance and development of the park through practical conservation work, fundraising for park facilities such as benches on the bowling greens and activities such as the Annual Community Fun Day held every September. According to the Ranger, the Friends group in Rhos is mainly made up of community councillors and people that are part of other groups as well. The Friends' treasurer is also the clerk of the community council. The volunteer-led programme is varied, offering live music events, family fun days, arts and craft activities and sports coaching. One measure of the success of local participation is that the park has been awarded Green Flag status for several years running. (The Green Flag Award® scheme recognises and rewards the best green spaces in the UK. 'Community involvement' is one of the eight criteria for the award.)

Crown green bowls, as distinct from flat green bowls, is closely associated with industrial towns and cities in the Midlands and northern parts of England and North Wales. According to Jackson (1968: 101), it was 'almost exclusively working class' and appealed particularly to older men. Bowls belonged to the same aspects of community as working men's clubs. He comments on the dynamics when a working-class group sets up a bowls club in a municipal park: the contrast between the officials who see the park as a public amenity and the players who 'want to build around the green the familiar, interlocking cells of community' (Jackson 1968: 109). Teams operate within a strong communal setting and spectators interact with players, providing advice and commentary.

The old Rhos Bowling Club which existed before the park refurbishment was successful in local competitions. Like the clubs described by Jackson, the team was all-male and the clubhouse was a male preserve. During the refurbishment programme, the members of the bowls team relocated to greens in the neighbouring villages. The team did not return en bloc when the two greens reopened. The Ranger describes a process of 'drifting back' but not to the previous state of affairs. The main initiative to re-launch in 2009 came from a group of women (some with previous experience of bowling as members of the Women's Institute) who "just wanted everybody … we wanted people to come in and enjoy what they were doing" (Hilda). In the same year, the Club successfully applied to the Community Council's Community Chest Fund for a grant for 'loan equipment' for use by the community. The Bowls is now organised by the Ponciau Banks Park Bowls Club, which has both male and female members. This gave rise to the distinction sometimes made between 'old Rhos' and 'new Rhos' among the players:

> 'all the ladies that play, they've only been coming here for about four years and they are the new Ponciau Banks Bowling Club. The men that are drifting back now played for Rhos years ago, and they either gave up bowls at the time or they went to another club.' (Ranger)

The competitive A team now has a majority of men but includes two female players. The B team mainly consisting of retirees plays 'because they want to meet people and spend time outdoors'. The Ranger describes the scene the previous week: "I counted up, and I figured there to be about 50 older people outside either playing bowls or watching the bowls." During the season, the team compete every other Tuesday afternoon, although they also meet some Wednesday afternoons and some weekday evenings. There is no youth section, but in summer 2015, with the help of the sports development section of Wrexham Council, and a community grant to buy child-sized bowls, the Park arranged taster days for schoolchildren with coaches from among the adult bowlers who received training.

The club premises is a small single-storey building overlooking one of the greens. Under the terms of the HLF/Council funding the current building is used for community activities as well. It serves as the clubhouse, a multi-use learning centre, polling station and accommodation for private hire for events like birthday parties. When the Ranger described the numbers at bowls in the previous quote, she also remarked that "inside there was about the same amount of young children in and out doing crafts ... quite a hive of activity". However, the sense that the building belongs to the bowling club remains among some of the older members, who pay a club subscription and recall the time when they could use the old building as an exclusive recreational space, "where [men] came in here and had a pint, and read the paper, and went and got themselves some fish and chips for lunch. And pretty much spent all day here, I think". This is no longer the case but there are echoes of the old attitudes in claims to the right to have keys to the building.

The Ranger describes how the present phase of funding is beneficial for participation in bowling activities because the costs of staffing and maintenance are largely covered by the HLF grant, in its seventh year of ten-year funding at the time of writing. Bowling has temporary protection from the cuts which have fallen on other areas of council spending. The future beyond the two-and-a-half-year horizon is uncertain. Grant schemes (especially those related to 'healthy living') may continue to be a source of income and it is unlikely that the council will withdraw all funding for park maintenance. But a greater share of the costs of being involved in bowling may fall on individual members: "So it might be that in two or three years' time the bowling club in Rhos might have to look after their own greens. At the moment they've got a gardener to do that ... they're very lucky," says the Ranger.

Bowling is clearly a well-established site of associational life in Rhos which has been through two main incarnations, reflected in the change of name after the park refurbishment. Today, the patterns of participation in the activities of the bowling greens in Ponciau Banks Park and the club building have to be considered in the light of the funding regime, namely the HLF grant which has helped to sustain the whole park, including the bowling greens, as an important centre of community, associational and self-organising activity. The HLF grant is administered by the Borough Council, which employs key staff to animate community activities and attract further grants, as well as to manage the space. The local authority is a key player but there are complex intersections between the 'civic' and the 'civil' at the very local level. There are close personal and working links between council employees, elected representatives and volunteers. The Friends organisation is clear evidence of this symbiosis.

The Ranger interview contains many hints concerning the frictions which exist around these fuzzy boundaries: the different attitudes of older and younger generations of bowlers or the reasons for changing patterns of male and female participation. The reference to financial cuts is less pessimistic than might be expected but this interpretation is linked to the specific local circumstances of the Park (parks and greens in other villages are seen to play a less central role in the local community).

## *The Community Café*

The main religious associations in Rhos are the Anglican parish and numerous chapels of various denominations. They have suffered a steep decline in membership and attendance, and their ageing congregations support few of the educational, social or musical activities that they once did (see Davis et al 2021). This mirrors the situation that Bruce (2010) describes in his re-study of church and chapel religion in four Welsh localities that were the subject of community studies in the 1950s and 1960s. He attributes the decline to secularisation exacerbated by dwindling economic cohesion, a rising population of incomers, and the erosion of Welsh language and culture. That social cohesion remains stronger in Rhos than in the more isolated rural villages in Bruce's study may help to account for the frequent evocation of the religious past in local accounts. The Café, on the other hand, is a new, 'alternative' form of Christian activity, which is not directly connected with the chapel culture of Rhos. It operates outside of any conventional denominational structure. It occupies a double-fronted shop on the main street in Rhos and provides low-cost food and drink and hosts community events. It is a non-profit enterprise, very local in form, with a variety of funding support, including donations from local businesses, as well as Community Fund grants. The Café provides training for volunteers through accredited and non-accredited courses with Adult Learning and Communities for Work. It is a new hybrid form of association with a religious ethos offering 'spiritual readings' and 'services' on Sundays as well as providing training, coordinating volunteering and hosting other community activities. The traditional self-supporting chapel relies on family and local social networks, but this new entity emerged from the vision of an 'outsider' who mobilised sources of funding including Lottery grants, religious charities and volunteer help. It has relationships to a community church in the region but it is not locally embedded in same way as the chapels. It has links to the wider civil and civic spheres (for example Communities First, the programme supporting the Welsh Government's Tackling Poverty agenda in selected disadvantaged areas) which they do not have. The pastoral worker who leads the venture, describes her motivation in these terms: "For me, it wasn't about trying to evangelise ... it's just about doing good and just about enhancing people's lives at whatever level they're at."

This interview displays a number of interesting contrasts with an interview with the now elderly leader of a local Welsh chapel. His narrative is shaped by references to family and there is a long section on the unbroken continuity of generations of family members who were local chapel leaders. The line is clearly at risk of coming to an end with the present generation. While the narrative is full of religious themes, ranging from hymnbooks to baptism to communion, it is firmly set in the taken-for-granted world of the village (rather than doctrine, the denomination or religion versus secularity) and is summed up in the phrase: "The village is the important thing, work and the village you live in."

In contrast, the interview with the Café leader is more action-oriented, concerned with the nuts and bolts of running a multifaceted social enterprise and, at the same time, it uses religious language in a different way. It is the language of individualised spirituality, with references to counselling, individual healing and 'spiritual readings'. "It's taking spirituality out where everybody is and saying, you don't have to conform, this is what I'm seeing for you, if you choose, then that's fine" (Café leader). It suggests that the privatisation of religious belief and practice exists in tandem with a strong sense of social responsibility. The success of the venture over several years also suggests that this a model which can withstand some of the pressures of secularisation and the hollowing out of religious institutions which is evident in the chapel context.

### Nene *community newspaper*

The third example from Rhos is the Welsh-language community newspaper or *Papur Bro* (see Chapter 4). Produced by volunteers, *Papurau Bro* were born out of the Welsh language revival in the 1970s at a point when national Welsh-language papers such as the weekly *Y Cymro* were in decline (Hughes 2008: 53). *Nene* was no different, and was formed out of a committee set up in Rhos to revitalise the Welsh language which, incidentally, also campaigned successfully for a Welsh-medium school in the village. The first 12-page edition was published in 1978 and it has been published 11 times per year ever since, containing a mixture of local news – including births and deaths, events and reports from local groups within the Welsh-speaking community. Most copies are distributed locally by volunteers in Rhos, Ponciau, Penycae and Johnstown, with around 150 sent by post to a Rhos diaspora. Funding is from two main sources: sales and subscriptions, and grant funding from the Welsh Government which supports all 52 *Papurau Bro* across Wales. Some supporters suggest that these grants represent a loss of independence. But they illustrate that even hyper-local media exist in a space with relations to the state (as well as to the market, insofar as they fill a gap in the commercial newspaper sector). Ifor, the editor, whose biography is described in detail in Chapter 4, is relatively confident about the level of subscriptions and notes that people make donations above the annual rate – a sign of local solidarity in his view. Yet, as chronicled by Hughes (2008), *Nene*, like many similar publications within the traditional Welsh-speaking areas, is suffering from a slow decline in circulation but, more critically, from an ageing volunteer base with few plans for succession. *Nene*'s reach in terms of audience exceeds that of many local associations, but as discussed in Chapter 4, it depends almost entirely on a deeply loyal and focused but dwindling core operation. This theme of association leaders, ageing and succession is a recurring one among local associations. It cannot be reduced to the problem of 'finding the right person' to take over. To the extent that the Welsh language has become more recognised and embedded in education and other public institutions since the 1970s, *Nene*'s relationship to the language movement has implicitly changed. It follows that content, editorial policy and even the written language itself may require some rethinking.

### *The Stiwt*

The Miner's Institute, known as the Stiwt, is a large, iconic building in the centre of Rhos, opened in 1926 and funded by the Miner's Welfare Association and a levy on the wages of local miners. It was the focal point for activities combining education, culture and entertainment, offering a library, games room, theatre, cinema and rehearsal space. Its ethos was shaped by the twin influences of the mining industry and the chapels, which ensured that it adhered to values of temperance, at least to the late 1960s. The decline of both mines and chapels led to the demise of the Stiwt and its closure due to bankruptcy in 1977. The building decayed quickly and by 1985 was due to be demolished. The threat galvanised the community, and a successful 'Save the Stiwt' campaign eventually secured £4.7 million funding from the local authority, Heritage Lottery and fundraising activities to renovate the building (Ellis and Bolton 2016). The Stiwt reopened in 1990 as a Charitable Trust under voluntary management and is now primarily an arts venue supported by Wrexham Council, the Arts Council of Wales and Friends of the Stiwt. It continues to be prominent symbol of Rhos and supports a wealth of cultural and community activities, but with increased competition for local authority funding as well as low audience numbers for some events, its future is hardly guaranteed. The problems are twofold: the perpetual reliance on external funding (and the expertise to acquire it); and the recruitment and retention of volunteer managers to run the large and complex facility. The response to a recent appeal to restore the Stiwt clock shows that the people of Rhos still have the capacity to make an impact in their own right. The sense of attachment and nostalgia runs deep: 'because my whole family were colliers, the Stiwt means everything to me ... and when I heard the clock chiming again I was almost in tears' (local resident quoted in BBC, May 2019). The fund raised £22,000, including £2,500 from the local community council, exceeding the original target. The fund increased further with a £50,000 contribution from Cadw, the Welsh Government's historic environment service, and £25,000 from Wrexham Council. It suggests that there is ongoing potential for mobilisation in local place-based local networks. At the same time, it illustrates the relationality and mutuality between 'community' initiatives, local civic bodies, the local authority and national public entities.

Associations in Rhos, both old and new, give the appearance of being well grounded in the locality, having a strong sense of belonging, and a high level of commitment from their supporters. The bowling club is now distanced from its male, working-class origins, but it continues to play a role in local life. It maintains the sporting tradition, provides a space for interaction and mobilisation of activities across generations. Its success depends on the supportive civic infrastructure (the local authority parks service) and other, overlapping associations, not simply the commitment of local bowling enthusiasts. An issue for the future is whether a shift in the balance of funding and resources would alter the character of the bowling club, possibly shifting it towards an exclusive membership-centred organisation away from an inclusive, community-focused cluster of activities. The example of the Community Café is different in the sense that it is a novel form of association, not the continuation of an existing tradition. It has become established despite this, offering a 'social model' of religion that sits comfortably within local social networks and creates spaces for cross-generational interaction. It is noteworthy that the funding model is multi-stranded and adaptable, combining private donations, sales, company donations and grants from public sources. It responds to needs at a very local level (for food, training, minority integration). *Nene* on the other hand has the feeling of being a well-established and well-embedded institution, although it is actually only a generation old. Its support depends on both individual commitment to the Welsh language in the local context, and on government subsidy – a feature of many local associations that provide a public service. The combination of personal commitment (through giving and volunteering) and government support is clearly beneficial to *Nene*, but it can sometimes be a contested issue because of the conditions attached to grants. It has not been a matter of contention thus far. Competition from social media, which involves an entirely different audience and funding arrangements, and the uncertainties surrounding the leadership succession pose greater risks. The *Papur Bro* may belong to that category of associations which Putnam would see as becoming dis-embedded from the conditions which were responsible for their creation. The memory of 'old' Rhos is a driver for a number of civil society projects, but the evidence of associations that represent 'contemporary', non-traditional Rhos is more elusive. The Stiwt exemplifies the pull of the past in its 'heritage' role at the same time as it attempts to channel local effort towards new and younger audiences.

## Overton associations

As described in Chapter 3, the village of Overton, while being in a similar orbit relative to Wrexham, has many features which contrast with Rhos. Among the most noticeable of them is the plethora of local associations, apparently exceeding the number active in Rhos, which has a much larger population. Many have a shorter history than those in Rhos. Overton also has greater visibility in social media. The list of users of Overton village hall runs to nearly 50 different (but sometimes overlapping) organisations, with local associations ranging from the Women's Institute to sports organisations, charity and church meetings, as well as dance and music groups. Some types of association are present in both villages, but others only exist in Overton – such as the twinning association, the Overton Amblers walking group, the Community Growers and the Beer 'n' Blues Festival. The local free newspaper, *Overton Oracle*, is published monthly online, and volunteers distribute a print copy to each household in the village. In our survey, a high proportion of Overton respondents reported 'helping out' in the community (56 per cent) without being paid, while an even higher percentage reported being involved in 'a local campaign to change something' (70 per cent). These campaigns ranged from local bus services to environmental measures, to traffic speed curbing and housing development restrictions. Meeting venues include the village hall, Scout hut, church halls and school. There is no central building in Overton as imposing as the Stiwt in Rhos, except the ancient parish church. This is a matter of regret to some, who would like to see a main community hub or centre with facilities for everyone, including young people. The following examples illustrate some of the distinctive features of associational life in Overton.

### *The La Murette and Overton-on-Dee Twinning Association*

The twinning arrangements with a French commune in the Isère were set up in 1994 by the chair of the community council. Both partner villages are relatively small but exchanges have taken place annually for 25 years, involving a variety of cultural and recreational activities. Although an interest in French language is not a requirement for participation, it is evident that the 20 or so core participants are predisposed to be active in the association through their professional roles (in teaching for example), their international work experiences and their cultural capital. The secretary of the association, who is not originally from Overton, described her experiences of language learning at school, holiday jobs abroad, teaching English to foreign students and travel as preparing her for the role. She participated in the very first exchange visit but has only become more actively involved recently, in retirement. The association is funded through fundraising events (the annual wine tasting event is the most important), a grant from the community chest and individual contributions made by hosts. Every person within the parish of Overton, not just the village itself, is automatically a member and there are no membership fees. Motivations vary among the different participants. For families, there may be an interest in supporting children's French language learning or for retired people it may be a form of cultural tourism. There is an underlying aim to encourage cultural exchange and goodwill between people of different nations, which is combined with a sense of responsibility to encourage an outward-looking attitude. The secretary gives the example of an award to a student in the primary school who "has shown all the sort of citizenship qualities that we're looking for". The longevity and success of the twinning association depends on the openness of the village networks (meetings are open, anybody can attend) and the cultural and social capital that participants bring. Typically, they are graduates who have the desire to express their sense of belonging and citizenship through this local/international vehicle.

## Women's Institute

The Overton W.I. was founded in 1925 and continues to meet regularly and host a programme of events that includes sharing and developing skills, trips and visiting speakers. At the time of the study there were 25–30 members ranging from their forties to quite elderly members. The core group including the programme secretary and treasurer have been members for several decades and describe themselves as 'older people'. The W.I. is therefore an association with a long tradition in Overton and these core members have in common that they were born in or near the village into relatively poor families, were educated in the local school and went into (for their time) the typically feminine occupations of nursing, secretarial work and retailing. They volunteer and support a number of organisations as well as the W.I. This pattern is reminiscent of some of the working-class associations in Rhos, where members and leaders with 'old Rhos' backgrounds have a sense of belonging to the locality, which is an intrinsic motivation to participate. They lament the fact that "the younger people aren't coming up to replace that, you know, on the committees and things like the church and the chapel, they've gone down of course. The W.I., we're not getting such younger members you know". Some members have been on the committee for more than 20 years. They acknowledge that it is not really good for an organisation and link this problem of succession to the level of commitment to 'the community'. "The committee is, you know, all getting older and we're worried that there won't be quite the same community spirit that there is now". A full account of the local W.I. would need to include the founding in 2014 of a new branch, the Maelor Belles, which meets in nearby Penley. It is part of a new wave of more informal, modern W.I.s, with an emphasis on women from younger generations. It may have a different understanding of 'community', interests and participation – more mobile and loosely tied to place.

*Parish church*

The Anglican parish church in Overton is an historic building in the centre of the village, famous for its ancient yew trees. The rector at the time of the research was a former doctor who retired early to train for the ministry. Originally from a Welsh-speaking area in South Wales, his career involved wide-ranging mobility across cities in England and Wales before ending up in Wrexham. He expresses his attachment to the locality less in terms of belonging or upholding tradition than in terms of his role as minister, which he describes as to "encourage and empower" local people to contribute to the "life of the village". In practice, this means interacting at the local level with individuals and groups, playing a role in local civil society through formal events and associations, and sometimes operating in a civic capacity, for example in official commemorations like Remembrance Day. The 'levels' are closely interrelated. As well as regular church services, the wide range of routine activities includes a toddlers' group, Messy Church (a type of Sunday School), coffee mornings, a music group, bell ringing and a food bank. These activities are supported and run by local residents, about half of whom the rector describes as "new people", not those who would say "we've always done it this way". His account of his everyday role – "just walking around the village and it's about 50 per cent of the people will say hello to me" – conveys a sense of mutual recognition and informal solidarity. Yet he acknowledges that this is underpinned by a heavy administrative load and computer skills which allow the church to run a Facebook page and communicate its activities. Like many contemporary clergy, the rector has a non-stipendiary position and is effectively a 'volunteer', although he does not use this term. As one enduring association within the fabric of local civil society, the parish is connected with other denominations, especially the Methodist church, with village celebrations like harvest, with the Friends of St Mary's Church (a charity to preserve and support the building), and the local Church in Wales primary school. In a telling comment, the rector explains that the church stands for more than religion: the 'big life events' such as weddings and funerals call for collective participation. "They want to be recognised in the village, it's through the church it's done". And although the Church in Wales has been disestablished for 100 years, it also plays a civic role in the annual Remembrance ritual, both at Cenotaph and afterwards in the church, which, the rector explains, is the biggest attendance of the year, exceeding Christmas. The example of Overton parish church illustrates the complex linkages between individual motivation (whether religious or diffusely humanistic), institutional strategies, resources and collective symbols. In contrast with religious life in Rhos, the story in Overton is not shaped by a nostalgia or survival narrative (or by 'new' religious expression) but by a sense of confidence in the present and future. Not without irony, the rector notes the claim to be special or atypical, saying: "they have quite a high opinion of themselves and of the village". While there is clearly some justification for this view in the amount of participation compared with the size of the population, and there is more resilience in parish and diocesan structures than among the chapels, the church shares in the field of action which is subject to the changing dynamics of population, alliances and funding which apply to other associations in Overton.

*Community councillor*

The case of a local community councillor provides useful insights into issues of associations and attachment. She explains in her interview that she is an 'outsider' in the sense that she was born and grew up and developed her career elsewhere in the region. Following significant life changes in mid-career, she elected to move from Wrexham to Overton, explaining that conditions in Wrexham has deteriorated since she first moved there, and she had "just got fed up with the area". She says she "wanted to live somewhere pretty and somewhere small ... And I found this house and I was really pleased, yeah. It's very tiny, there's only one bedroom ... I thought, [Overton is] a lovely place to live". This is a clear example of the choice for 'elective belonging' (Savage 2010) but it does not account for participation in associations as such. Her pathway to participation is described in an anecdote about litter-picking. Soon after her arrival she noticed when walking around Overton that there was some litter that would not be too difficult to collect. The *Overton Oracle* carried an article around the same time about another resident who had started litter-picking using resources such as litter-picking tools and bags from Keep Wales Tidy. She contacted this resident and became a Litter Champion herself. She relates:

'One day he said to me, "Could you organise a community litter pick?" And I thought, oh, gosh, yes, all right then, I'll have to go and see the Community Council about this one. So I went to a Community Council meeting and asked them if they would approve of me organising a community litter pick, which of course they did. And so that was the first thing I got involved in. I've organised several, well, lots of them really since then, community litter-picks.'

The outcome was an invitation to become a local councillor and roles on a number of committees. It is consistent with the idea of elective participation that she speaks of herself as "someone who likes to keep busy" and prefers to instigate things rather than belong to groups. She is also active in other associations, including being the secretary of the Parochial Church Council and the Rotary Club. She is the bringer of social and cultural capital which is 'spent' mainly in the local area, in response to the needs and call of the community, rather than capital which is accumulated organically through years of belonging and naturally existing networks.

## Discussion

Analysis of the similarities and contrasts between the two localities has highlighted several themes of broader relevance to debates on local civil society and other socio-spatial contexts. Our key questions were about the range and depth of participation in local associations; their sustainability in terms of organisation and funding; and how changes in associational forms and the experiences of local civil society participants are shaped by local contexts. In answer to the first question, the evidence shows that complex forms of associational life exist in both localities, with high levels of participation. Both villages have a reputation for strong 'community' ties, but the stories are noticeably different in terms of their patterns of association. Rhos associations, with few exceptions, are longstanding, with direct lines of descent from the key institutions of the mining industry and the chapels. This is both a source of strength, as there is a widespread sense of obligation to recollect, preserve and maintain local traditions, but it is also a point of weakness as the generations which have direct family and institutional connections to the emblematic past are dying out. While it is not unusual for voluntary associations to be led and supported by older generations, the problem appears to be particularly acute in many Rhos associations. The reputation that Overton has for an unusual number of local associations seems well justified. Their relationship to the population of the village contains some elements of nostalgia for the historical past (as in the political history) but the overwhelming impression is that most associations have relatively recent origins and attract a mixture of participants with both old and incomer status, a distinction that does not appear to figure greatly in the dynamics of local organisation. A related question is whether participation in civil society has become increasingly stratified along lines of class and other axes of inequality. Physically and socially, Rhos remains a post-industrial and therefore working-class milieu. This governs the sense of place, where identity is strong because of belonging (understood in terms of being born and bred in Rhos, Welshness, Rhos dialect). In Overton, the more rural character and smaller size coincide with a population that is somewhat older, better qualified and healthier and wealthier than Rhos. It has more economic, social and cultural capital for investment and the phenomenon of 'elective belonging' provides the rationale for capital to be invested in local associations. The contrast between the villages suggests a positive answer to the question about inequality: it seems unlikely that conditions will lead to convergence in the foreseeable future.

One important theme is the ways that sources of funding are rearranging the roles and responsibilities of citizens, the state and society. The fundraising efforts of local associations may target individual donations, membership fees, grants and contracts, the National Lottery and may include earned income. Our study provides examples of how these choices are affecting their operations and sustainability. The case of the bowling activities in Ponciau Banks Park shows how complex they can be. Wrexham County Borough Council manages the bowling greens and the park, which was the beneficiary of a grant from the HLF. The authority employs the Park Ranger. Local associations are vital in raising money to run Annual Community Fun Days and providing equipment such as benches on the bowling greens. Members of the local community may request a financial grant from the Community Chest Fund administered by the local authority to assist their organisation, local group or charity (for example, the Bowling Club's grant for loan equipment for use by the community). A 'friends' group, the Friends of Ponciau Banks raises money to spend on the park's facilities and activities. Volunteers contribute to the upkeep of the park with path maintenance, weed clearing, painting and working with school groups. This represents a civil society ecosystem with coalitions of interest, overlapping and hybrid organisations, grassroots activities, intermediaries and service providers. The local ecosystem may even have international ramifications. The history of Rhos shows that it was open to international volunteering in the 1930s. There is no direct equivalent today, but international cooperation may be expressed in other ways – for example by overseas concert tours by the male voice choirs (Owen 2009). In this chapter, the evidence of associational life in both villages is presented as being overwhelmingly positive, but a cautionary note should be sounded. Some aspects of local civil society are capable of being isolating, exclusionary or even uncivil. This is evident, for example, in the opposition among some Overton residents to new housing developments, or the reluctance in Rhos to share its traditions with new types of incomer. However, the civil society ecosystem is an open system which can adapt to changes in the economic, social and political environment. The diversity and interdependence mostly engender cooperation and trust. Associations in Overton are generally less reliant on the local state for funding. The community council is an important intermediary but facilities such as the village hall, the playing fields, playground and public toilets (Dallimore 2016) are not funded by Wrexham Council. Nothing involves external funding (National Lottery, Welsh Government or Arts Council) on the scale that is required for the Stiwt in Rhos. Overton is therefore better placed for civil society associations to be sustainable in the prevailing climate of austerity in public funding and public services.

## Conclusion

In Chapter 1 we posed the question: where does the array of small-scale clubs and societies fit into the concept of civil society? We studied the patterns of associational life in the two villages in order to provide some answers. Clearly, local associations are organised expressions of solidarity which are part of a multi-layered arrangement of state, market and private relations. Associations are neither fully independent nor dependent on any of these elements, but their influence is always felt in terms of regulation, funding and legitimacy. The patterns of association in Rhos and Overton cannot be understood without referring to the powerful influences of the economic austerity policies of the last decade, the political ideology of social solidarity and voluntarism captured by the notion of 'big society', and the need for belonging where collective ties have been attenuated. Yet, overwhelmingly, the evidence underlines the importance of the local. Not because geography determines the pattern of social relations; this idea of social or community relations corresponding to specific geographical milieux or scales was rejected earlier. And not because the two villages somehow 'fit' into an order defined by social class, occupation, culture or social capital. It would be possible, but misleading, to distinguish between types of participation such as civic, or 'municipal', in contrast to a community or social enterprise model. A classification of this type would break down with the messiness of the field of locally orientated action. The striking contrasts between participation in Rhos and Overton are, rather, the product of actions, goals, types of sociability and experiences over time which reflect their different alignments to the state and for-profit sectors, as well as their local resources for building civil society.

# 6

# The entwining of civil society, economy and state at local levels

In theoretical discussions, civil society is conceptually distinct from economy and the state. Local empirical studies, however, show that civil society is shaped by the economic and political relations that determine the nature of participation and the direction of civil society actions, along with their organisation and impact. In other words, both state and economy are constitutive of the local environment in which civil society evolves and operates. In this final empirical chapter, we highlight the structural elements which link individual civil society participation with the wider context of economy and the state as we consider these structural aspects a vital part of empirical analysis. Continuing with the biographical approach, we broaden the analysis to discuss the civil society relations with the local economy and institutions associated with the state, their impact on individual lives as well as the wellbeing of local communities. This approach is focused on embodied attachments, such as individual accounts of participation over time and mutual understandings of the norms of civility and solidarity, which frame the unique balance between local community interests and individual understandings of what constitutes a 'good and fulfilled life'. We point towards specific patterns of resource mobilisation and institutional support that can effectively support the action-field of civil society, or disrupt the balance of interests, thus harming local civil society initiatives.

We begin by discussing the role of embodied attachments that structure the field of civil society action, such as age, gender and social class. The second part then outlines four biographical cases from Rhos and Overton to illustrate the relevance of these embodied attachments in the analysis of links between local economy, institutions and civil society participation. The third section is an analysis of civil society practices that utilise the economic base to facilitate participation. Finally, there is an analysis of the impact of state institutions and policy agendas on participation in local civil society.

## Stratification in the context of civil society participation

To explore the interlinkages between actors and local social structures, we focused on 'embodied attachments' (Savage et al 2005: 53) that map a variety of connections between individual biographies and the broader social structures. These embodied attachments link places and new solidarities as well as the potential for collective actions, with the everyday experiences of participation, civility and belonging, thus framing the social field of civil society to support, or deny support to, specific types of social actions. In the empirical data we observed three broad stratification patterns relating to the analysis of civil society participation and its links with the local economy and state institutions.

## Civil society across the life cycle

Participation in local civil society in our research sites depends on the availability of free time that can be allocated to social activities on top of the individual's economic activities. Time availability varies significantly between different biographical stages of life (Lancee and Radl 2014). Childhood and youth facilitate participation via educational institutions as well as family socialisation. Such initiatives involve young people in the community structures and teach them about the rules of community collaboration. In Wales, for example, the Welsh Baccalaureate foundation level qualification requires young people to spend 15 hours on active community participation (Welsh Joint Education Committee (WJEC) 2016). The analysis of biographical cases which follow in this chapter highlight in particular the importance of these types of community engagement as a foundation for building norms of civility and solidarity. In the biographical period of adulthood, pockets of free time that can be contributed to community engagements become limited. Work and family commitments take priority over community participation, and the links with institutions which previously facilitated community engagement relax. The forms of participation reflect the patterns of time associated with leisure, such as fitness activities or interests, and classes organised in the evenings and weekends, rather than throughout the day. These limitations on free time and the selective nature of activities reinforce limited availability and access to participation. The lower priority of these activities, especially compared with work and family demands, puts individuals more often in the position of passive consumers rather than active participants. This position restricts access to decision-making structures and limits the representation of this age group in local civil society activities.

The biographical stage of life associated with retirement and older age signals the return of participation and civil society commitments (Jones and Heley 2016). Once more, increased availability of free time allows for an intensification of participation at the local level. This age group usually has more time, commitment and skills to build associations and initiatives from the grassroots. These collective actions often reflect the interests and relevance of particular individuals and conform to the 'dominant status' thread (Smith 1983) that sees participation in local civil society dominated by groups with particular socio-economic profiles. Nonetheless, across our research sites this did not mean that conformity to the dominant status of actors being male, middle-aged, high-income (Smith 1994) always held true. This is the case in Rhos, where the biographically significant aspects of the older generation are centred around working-class mining heritage, and this aspect becomes a leading narrative in local civil society activities. The continuous fight for survival of the Miner's Institute or heritage activities related to the local mines illustrate this point. This stratification across age and generations may lead to a lack of representation and forms of exclusion in participation where civil society as a field of action favours the interests of older generations and excludes the younger members of the community, perhaps with the exception of sport activities. In Overton, this generational divide has led to the organisation of two separate Women's Institutes representing different expectations and fulfilling different needs between women of different ages.

## Gendered economic relations

In both research sites, Rhos and Overton, we observed that participation in local civil society is gendered. Local civil society often reproduces distinctions between male and female activities and responsibilities, reflecting gendered interests, and structuring activities to accommodate the different patterns of free time (Cnaan et al 1996). Among associations, gender is a significant aspect of sports activities, for example in Rhos, where only recently in the context of a previously male club the Ponciau Banks Park Bowls Club introduced a female competitive team, or in the strong presence of Zumba classes in the community centres across both villages. Gender-based associations, such as the Women's Institute or all-male choirs, are common features of the historic local civil society landscape. The shift to gender-mixed activities is more prevalent in new associations, based around environmental and healthy living issues.

The exceptional case of civil society participation associated with gender is the period of motherhood. This stage of life, where maternity care gives women pockets of time outside of economic activities, has been found to be restricted by duties of caring for very young children (Lancee and Radl 2014). Nonetheless, motherhood also creates the social and cultural space to re-enter the local civil society structures and opens up opportunities to get to know other mothers and the wider community. These mother-centred networks form along the lines of shared experience and create the bedrock of support networks that can be transformed into more institutionalised forms of local civil society, such as childminding networks, playgroups, the Scout movement, and children's activities and classes. This element of local civil society builds into the pre-school and school educational systems that cater for the younger members of the community, into local council structures in terms of management and regulations, as well as the network of economically valuable local businesses and third sector organisations focused on childcare and education.

## Class and place

The last significant pattern of participation observed in Rhos and Overton focuses on the broader economic landscape of the places. This includes physical wealth, reflected in property prices as well as the people who live in and choose to engage with the place. We focused on a 'socially constructed, embedded process in which people reflexively judge the suitability of a given site as appropriate given their social trajectory and their position in other fields' (Savage et al 2005: 12). Where the place is associated with a specific industry, such as coal mining in Rhos, it incorporates related symbols and practices into the identity of the local civil society organisations. It builds on memories of the past and heritage to uphold continuity and create a sense of belonging to the larger narrative that is often aligned with elements of the social class system, such as working-class solidarity build on experiences of work in mines. By contrast, places such as Overton build their place identity around more middle-class references to the 'estate-village' that represents idealised community and the concept of a 'closed village' (Short 1992; see also Chapter 3). This idea of Overton's uniqueness and authenticity is strongly present in protest against new developments and any interference in the image of the place.

Additionally, the local civil society organisations draw upon the availability of individual skills and local knowledge. The issue of free time was discussed earlier, but also not without impact is the know-how of people who have acquired high-level skills in organisations and professional employment over many years. Skilled in reaching and linking into networks beyond their local community, into local businesses as well as councils, these people galvanise local civil society into collective actions that go beyond recreational activities and into expressions of new local solidarities and civic belonging.

## Biographies of civil society in action

Within these broad participation patterns, we identify four illustrative biographical accounts, two from Rhos and two from Overton. Our aim is to explore the complexities of embodied social relations in the context of specific civil society actions as they unfold within individual biographies. These four case studies highlight the relationship between biographically relevant social actions and their multi-level links with the economy and the state's institutional framework. From these four cases we have drawn the biographical patterns of civil society participation that unfold over time and build the patterns of social solidarities and civility.

## William's case: the mining heritage of Rhos

William's biography reflects the pervasive influence of Rhos' mining heritage. As a retired miner, his life story is full of male camaraderie and a working-class work ethic that illustrates the wider intersections of class and gender. For William, mining is not merely a work environment; it is a way of life that has shaped family relationships, educational opportunities and leisure activities. In his life story narrative, William, 70 years old at the time, emphasises that his father was also a miner, but he lived only with his grandmother in Rhos and attended school and chapel. William did not finish school, which at that time was not that uncommon. Instead, he went to a labour exchange, where he was asked about his father's occupation, and the following week he started working in the local Hafod mine. William says: "Because you were the son of a miner, the job was open to you." The mining profession in Rhos was reproduced over generations: sons were expected to follow in their fathers' footsteps, and their 'right' to this employment was traditionally enforced by unions. This institutional protection for miners as an occupational group assured job security, a relatively stable income and contributed to a way of life that defined the identity of Rhos and its people.

William enjoyed working at the mine. His stories of employment are full of joy and mischief. He received appropriate training, shared hardship with other miners, but also developed a strong bond, a camaraderie with his colleagues of the kind widely reported in the sociological literature on mining (Dennis et al 1956). He says: "The friendships that you had in the pit, I'd never known it anywhere else." William mentions that he was buried and rescued twice and explains that risk was just part of the job. The fact that these risks were shared with others fuelled a sense of solidarity and mutual responsibility. During his career as a miner, he worked in several different pits. He describes the working conditions and security measures, getting up at half past four in the morning and coming back late in the evening after a visit to the pub. William mentions: "the friendships that we had in the pit was that someone would be looking after you, and it wouldn't be just one, it would be everybody. Everything was fun, you know." The sense of community, built around the mining occupation, accommodated the miners' lifestyle and included major social institutions, such as pubs and chapels. In the meantime, he met his wife and settled into family life, eager to be a part of the mining village of Rhos.

When the economic situation of mining in the UK changed dramatically, William took an active role in the struggle against the economic changes that affected his way of life and threatened the wellbeing of Rhos. This part of his life story is dominated by the miners' strikes which took place in the pits across Wales in 1984–85. William tells us that he was one of a few Rhos miners who went to the picket line, and he took part in protests in London. In his story, William mentions that industrial action against mine closures had challenged the sense of solidarity among the miners and caused some difficulties within the community itself, but he claims that this produced no lasting divisions. William says:

> 'men wanted to go back to work and, well, we had no choice, we had to let them through. But we still laugh about it when we talk about it today, because it was the best summer we ever had. We did without, but we're still here today to tell the story about it, you know.'

The active struggle against the economic changes threatening the existence of the way of life with which William grew up is one of the critical points in his biographical account. There is a sense of joy in the struggle, of being part of something bigger, civil society taking a stand against the political authority and economic threat. William says:

> 'We had to stay out on strike, because to be honest I thought we'd have won. And that's why I stayed on strike. Until there'd come a time that I couldn't do any more than what I did, you know, I had to go back to work. But nobody ever called anybody a scab or anything like that.'

William says that the year-long industrial action was financially very difficult for him and his family. At that point, he had two children. They were living on donations from strike supporters and the unions, and, in the process, he was arrested for begging while collecting donations. This part of his biographical narrative highlights the processes of economic mobilisation. People on the picket lines were supported by their community members at large, tapping into the economic resources at the local level that allowed them to continue their civil society activities for a year. In the long term, however, William mentions that the situation put a strain on his marriage as well as on others in the community. Men did not bring money home. There was a sense of a lack of order in the community, with too many men forced to be idle. Under pressure, William decided to finish his strike. With a sense of loss, he explains: "Because we'd lost by then, and it was something that I'll live with it, and I was proud that I did it, you know, and it was for your rights at the end of the day. If I hadn't done it, I think I would be worse than what I am today."

The failure of the miners' strike, however, led to a new opening in William's biographical project. He managed to transform his biographical experiences and engage in new forms of local social action that embraced the generations-old traditions of Rhos as a mining village and his memories of the times of turmoil and social change. After the mines closed in 1986, William briefly worked for the council and then experienced serious health issues. As he retired, he got involved with the local mine heritage group that is partially supported by the council. He now guides tours through the mines, makes school trips and tells younger generations about the life and work in the pits, thus preserving what is left of the proud past of the area's mining industry. William says:

> 'You know, it is an education to us, because we never thought of a child's view of it, you know, but you get to the school, and they enjoy it ... children take it all in, you know. You think they are not listening but they are. And I wouldn't have thought by going into a pit that I would be telling children about the strike.'

William speaks about his youth with fondness and enthusiasm, but he knows that his work now is about preserving the memory of the mining culture and sharing the legacy of their lost attempt to preserve it from the broader economic changes.

William's biography illustrates multiple engagements with local civil society. The history of the strikes exemplifies the struggle against political actions to close down the mines and his commitment to 'the pits', and the heritage work aims to negotiate the new relationship between Rhos' economic past and its uncertain future. William's sense of identity and belonging links with the reality of the post-mining village, and his biographical activism is anchored in the preservation of the memory and culture of 'the pits'.

## Cai's case: the Rhos Christmas Panto

The second biography based in Rhos comes from Cai, a 53-year-old media personality, who now lives in Cardiff. Cai is younger than William, and his biography shows different aspects of community dynamics. It focuses on the arena of Welsh language and Rhos' unique culture. This story illustrates the intersecting aspects of economic deprivation and loss of employment opportunities between generations, with the unique sense of place and rich cultural heritage. Cai was born in Rhos, and his parents ran a shop, which gave him a special insight into Rhos' social life. From a very early age, he was interested in arts and drama. Cai mentions that his aunt was a well-known opera singer, and Rhos was home to a well-respected dramatics society and several Welsh choirs. The school he attended encouraged participation in arts activities – he wrote plays, acted, directed and produced. The only place where he could not get a role was the dramatic society, because he did not get along with the director. In hindsight, this taught him about rejection and perseverance in this profession:

> 'I've got a very love/hate relationship with the area, it's the sort of area that if you fail, they're very, very unforgiving and if you succeed, they are very, very supportive. I always felt that everybody in the village thought that there was something special about them ... I think it's because culturally because of music and drama and something to do with – and I don't know whether it's confidence, or whether it's lack of confidence disguised as confidence, the village people tend to be quite big characters, especially the women.'

In contrast to William, Cai sees Rhos through the lens of female-driven participation, giving us an insight into a different side of Rhos. The artistic environment that nurtured his creativity and freedom of expression was a springboard to his future career in entertainment. After school, he chose to study dramatic arts in London. From there he started a very successful career in entertainment and embraced his own identity as a gay man. Cai never returned to live in Rhos, but the village still features strongly in his private and professional life. His family and close friends are still living in Rhos, and he visits often. He sees the changes on the street, the general sense of decline, but he also actively searches for a way to revive the old Rhos with its vibrant arts and culture.

Professionally, Cai is leveraging his position to bring Rhos' cultural heritage, such as drama and choirs, into the broader Welsh mainstream. He uses his expertise and position in cultural institutions, such as S4C (the Welsh-language television channel) to showcase Rhos in the national context. As a consequence, Cai galvanises local social action and draws in necessary resources to support Rhos' arts and culture. In two televised shows he introduced viewers to the dramatics scene by organising a showing of the Christmas Panto ('Seren Nadolig Rhos' in 2011) and conducting a choir, which won a national choir competition. When talking about his motives, he says:

> 'I went back to my village to create a new theatre society, to recreate what I had in my childhood, and their challenge was to put on, in three months, they had to put on their own production of pantomime, and that was going out on television, that was an absolute pure pleasure.'

Both of the shows brought together the people of Rhos. They celebrated the arts, through drama and singing, which has been there for generations. Cai mobilised community participation, and the majority of work came from the people of Rhos, especially those who were Welsh-speaking. The groups involved in the process kept going even after the shows finished, and both the choir that won a national competition and the drama society operate in Rhos to this day.

Cai's story illustrates the biographical relevance of links between sense of belonging, even if only sentimental, and the civil society field of social actions. Cai is now using his established position and professional expertise to support the community that shaped who he is today. He is able to mobilise resources from the wider state-based institutional framework supporting Welsh culture, such as the Welsh Language Board (active between 1993 and 2012) and Welsh-language-speaking media outlets. There is no doubt that Cai feels very strongly about the future of Rhos and the future of arts in Rhos in particular. At the same time, he recognises that he has outgrown Rhos. In his biographical interview, Cai says:

'My village will always have a very special place in my heart and so will its people, but I, personally I wouldn't – never say never, personally at this moment in time, I could not envision myself ever moving back to live there because the village has got very little to offer me personally ... I think Rhos now suffers from being a very big village. If it was a small town, I have a feeling it would sit more comfortably and there would be room for various societies within it to flow among each other.'

Cai's story is a strong example of the mobilisation of local civil society by a person with deep roots in the community, but from afar. Cai is negotiating his sense of belonging to the specific place, understood in terms of cultural heritage and unique Welshness, with the economic realities of contemporary Rhos and uses his personal and professional skills to engage with the state-based support structures that can preserve this unique version of Rhos' cultural heritage.

## Susan's case: the issue of new development in Overton

Susan's biographical interview is the first of two to represent Overton. Susan has lived in Wrexham borough for most of her life but moved to Overton at the time of her retirement, and she is now an Overton community councillor. Her biographical narrative illustrates the intersection of gender and age that frames participation in Overton's local civil society and incorporates elements of state institutions into civil society actions.

Susan was born close to Liverpool. Her family moved to Wigan when she was six, and then at the age of 11 they moved again to live in a village near Wigan. She went to college in Bath, where she trained as a home economics teacher. She met her husband while hitchhiking. She had one child, and after that, she did not go back to teaching. The young family moved to Wrexham, and she opened a homebrew shop producing real ale. She had some success in business, but due to the heavy work, her health deteriorated to the point that she closed her business. She lived in Wrexham for 37 years, and during that time, her marriage collapsed. In a search for a new life, she bought a small cottage in Overton. Susan arrived in Overton as a single women, with adult children. This gave her enough personal time to get engaged with the community and use some of her business experience and skills.

Susan's involvement with Overton's civil society started with her own action of picking up litter. In her narrative, she explains:

> 'And because I've been busy, I'm just a busy person, I don't sit still, I don't watch television very often. And I just like keeping busy really. So one of the things I noticed when I was walking – this was the first thing I got involved with in Overton. One of the things I noticed when I was walking around Overton was the fact that there was a bit of litter around … I thought, well, that wouldn't be difficult to [deal with] … I could go around with a carrier bag every morning and pick this up … I contacted Keep Wales Tidy and they came to see me and I became a Litter Champion, and then one day they said to me, "Could you organise a community litter pick?" And I thought, oh, gosh, yes.'

This initiative emphasises Susan's individual interest in keeping the outdoors tidy and addressing problems that she felt able to handle. In her narrative Susan mentions that litter was always something that bothered her, but in Wrexham, where she lived previously, the scale of the problem was beyond her abilities and means. In Overton, her individual resources, such as time and her physical ability to undertake the project, were sufficient to get involved. Her own actions sparked interest and support in the wider community. She attended community meetings and with time became a community councillor. She is involved in an abundance of music, walking and gardening groups that represent a variety of associations and interest groups in Overton. She stresses that her interest is in the community and that none of these activities are political. She sees her role as an enabler and organiser for the expansion of community life in Overton. However, when the local county council proposed a plan for a new housing development that would affect the 'village community' and strain community resources, she was one of the people who expressed their concerns in the consultation process. She points out that:

> 'A lot of people are set against any development. A lot of people are set against the scale of the development, yes, they were frightened, a lot of people were frightened by it, but we [the council] managed to calm them down a little bit and say – it is not going to happen like

that and probably won't happen ... for the years to come yet ... But just fill in the consultation form and wait for the results.'

This process of consultation is the institutional framework set up to allow the community stakeholders to express their interests in or opposition to proposed changes, such as local developments, school and library closures. As a councillor, Susan uses this framework to channel the community resistance to changes, ensuring that the voice of the community is heard, at least for now. Susan is well embedded in the local community council and can use her professional skills as well as time to address local problems, such as the closing of public toilets, maintenance of public pathways as well as a possible library closure. Her energy and commitment to the village and community is a driving force which helps local civil society to prosper in Overton. She is in the stage of life that allows her more time and freedom to participate in local civil society and use her considerable skills and business acumen to succeed in Overton's community structures and lead a number of social and cultural initiatives. Her relationship with Overton focuses on the size of the place. In her reasoning, if a village is small enough, you will be invited into the civil society activities merely by being around. This feature of Overton invites civil society engagement that expands toward both local political structures, such as her appointment to the community council as well as economic and social structures that secure civil society control and oversight over the community resources that facilitate community participation.

## Karen's case: motherhood in Overton

The second biographical case linked to Overton is Karen's. This case illustrates the type of civil society participation that is embedded in gender relations, especially the period of motherhood, and the institutional structures supporting community childcare and education. Karen, who was 66 years old at the time of the interview, was born in England. Her father was an engineer, and her mother was taking care of three children. She became pregnant when she was 17 and was married early to her school friend. When Karen was 20 and pregnant again, she was involved in a car accident with her husband. She was in a coma for a month, and her husband died. Karen gave birth to her daughter a few months later. She was grieving, living next to her parents and raising two kids. She remarried and, together with her husband, decided to buy the local post office from family friends and run her own business. In the meantime, they had two more sons and decided to search for a bigger house while the post office closed. They drove through Overton to visit a friend and found the right house for the whole family.

As a young mother, new to the village, she was taken under the wing of an older neighbour, who introduced her to the parent and toddlers group and people in the chapel. A local GP who was pregnant at the time asked if she would be interested in childminding for her, and within a few weeks she was officially registered as a childminder. Karen recognised that childcare provided a niche opportunity in Overton and the wider area and that there was limited information and supply of childcare services. In her narrative, she describes the process:

> 'But me being me, I couldn't just childmind, so I then started to find out who else childminded around here, was there a list? So I joined NCMA and they were keen to set up small groups, so I started Wrexham Childminding Group in the library in Wrexham. We run our own vacancy list, our own buggy hire, cot hire, highchair hire, anything that somebody was short of and because I had this big garage [laughs] everything was stored there.'

Within eight years, Karen was involved in setting up Child Protection training and took a paid position as a development worker with NCMA (National Childminders Association) for the area. She used her business skills and ability to pull in institutional support for childcare to set up a network for mothers, young families and children. Karen mentions:

> 'From the day I arrived in the village, because I had got a child playgroup age and a younger one toddler age, so the mums run the toddler group, so we got involved with that. I got dragged into the committee of the playgroup, because I'd worked with money, I was given the treasurer's job and it just went on from there. And I've actually followed the children as they've gone on, I'm still involved with our playgroup even now.'

During her time, she was involved in several local initiatives, such as safety inspections of playground equipment, fundraising for a park and organising junior discos. She was growing frustrated with the community council, as in her view it was catering to the older rather than the younger population. To make a change she ran for office in a by-election and became a community councillor. She stayed in that position for another 25 years. She is engaged in most civil society events in Overton, such as the Blues and Real Ale Festival, the Women's Institute, Scout's Hut. The council also manages the Village Hall which they bought with a Lottery grant that is the base for several civil society groups and initiatives. She is now slowly "letting the younger generation take over". Karen's participation in Overton's civil society structures highlights important gender aspects that reflect broader connections between the place and the individual. Her position as a young mother, mentored by other older female friends, was the institutional pathway into the community. It allowed her to use the biographical stage of motherhood to participate and later on organise participation in this particular aspect of community life. The connections and position provided her springboard to achieve the position of community councillor, from where she could draw on both economic and political structures to mobilise local civil society.

## Linking economy and state with the analysis of civil society participation

Links with the local economy, such as opportunities for employment and commerce, form the foundations of community life. Directly linked to the economic wellbeing of local communities is access to individual and community resources that will affect the ability of local groups to mobilise into collective action. The empirical links between economic resources and civil society participation can be found within the biographical narratives that detail the individual accounts of partaking in civil society actions. They can be observed across three broad aspects of community life: the impact of and reaction to broader macro-economic changes, the emergence of local entrepreneurship initiatives, and the formation of a network of economic solidarities.

## Civil society as reaction to economic change

The first link between civil society participation and the local economy is a corollary of the existential embeddedness of local civil society structures in the broader context of the global, national and regional economy. Economic activities, such as access to the labour market, as well as their dependency on macro-economic factors, determine population movement between places, access to individual resources and community infrastructure. These economic relations become entwined with the identity of places as well as individual biographies. To this day, places such as Rhos and Overton carry the marks of previous economic relations, such as Rhos' mining heritage and the estate village of Overton, that have shaped their local history and built a sense of identity that incorporates the place's occupational character, socio-economic, generational and gender hierarchies. As much as the organisation of civil society reflects the economic landscape, it is especially interesting to observe how civil society actions are used to protect and preserve these economic relations against the impact of macro-economic changes.

In the case of Rhos, the example of the miners' strikes illustrates civil society resistance towards mine closures which threatened the way of life built around occupational identities and economic relations. William's account of that time highlights long-term mobilisation and individual sacrifice to resist the changes, while also noting tensions within the community about the nature of these civil society actions. He highlights the disagreements with those who crossed the picket lines, the problems with men left 'idle', and the difficulties within impoverished families, along with the sense of engagement and empowerment stemming from the feeling of being part of a bigger social movement. Even after the strikes failed to stop the mine closures, the experience of participation had a long-lasting biographical significance for William. It transformed his engagement in the strikes into a biographical project devoted to preserving the memory of both the events and the way of life that had been brought to an end. In the case of Overton, a similar threat to the cohesion and identity of the community was posed by the proposal of extensive housing development. At the core of the community's fears lay the unpredictability of the expansion, including the influx of people as well as the strain on public services that would directly affect their perceived way of life. The response, as narrated in Susan's biographical interview, followed more institutional patterns of formal consultation, channelling the unrest in the community to express their resistance to the idea.

What both cases have in common is a change in the locality's economic relations, either by the withdrawal or inflow of substantial capital, that elicits a sense of threat to the community's way of life and sense of belonging. The rapid changes in the population make-up caused by either the inflow or outflow of people threatens established solidarities as well as the norms of civility, challenging individual attachments that have been developing over a significant time. The reaction to these changes, so different in both cases, corresponds to the perceived level of threat. The miners' strikes were directly related to tangible threats to the economic wellbeing of the families and villages. In contrast the more moderate form of resistance, participation in a consultation process, was built around discontent towards investment that potentially threatened the way of life, but not the entire economic wellbeing of the community. In both cases, the broader economic change elicited civil society responses, pointing toward civil society's role in protecting the established ways of life, sometimes even after the battle is lost, like in the remarkable case of William.

## Local entrepreneurship: generating and pulling in external resources

The second link between civil society and the local economy is associated with instances of local entrepreneurship, which includes opportunities and activities that create value for the broader local community as well as specific individuals. These activities would include the initiatives of individuals who identify a specific need within their community and are able to mobilise economic resources and community support to organise a civil society response. This aspect of civil society participation is driven by a commitment to improvements and recognition of what constitutes 'value' to the local community. Local entrepreneurship can be found in all biographical cases presented earlier, but two accounts of civil society participation – Karen's childminding activities in Overton and Cai's continuous efforts to organise the high-profile cultural engagements and bring attention to the Stiwt – clearly highlight the links between the local economy and civil society participation.

With her childminding activities, Karen's case shows how individuals identify a niche or a problem within community services and undertake action to address it. As a young mother taking care of her children, Karen was asked to provide childcare for another working mother. She recognised the need within the community to provide childcare, which by extension was also her individual source of income. More importantly, however, she identified the difficulties associated with organising childminding provision. Karen thus organised a network of childminders, connected them with young mothers, became an information hub regarding childminding registration and regulations, and organised an exchange platform for baby products, such as buggies and cots. All these activities that provide value for the broader community were developed on top of her economic activities as a childminder and then evolved into a professional interest, as she was asked to develop that type of services further.

Her narrative also illustrates how self-help – in Karen's case to tackle maternal isolation – can become a welfare service supporting child development, and eventually institutionalised as regulated childcare. This in turn, can become a cornerstone of the local economy, supporting many women in employment. Although not unique, childcare is an important case study in what might be termed 'co-produced welfare' (Pestoff 2006). In Wales, around a third of all childcare services are managed by local voluntary groups creating a model that differs from the consumer-led or state-sponsored model followed in many other countries. Local people (mainly parents) participate in providing economic support (paying fees and fundraising) to groups, they engage politically in management and wider governance, and in many cases also provide pedagogical support. Co-production sees the state providing varying amounts of funding and monitoring quality by regulation. Such citizen participation at the micro level or site of production of welfare services corresponds with calls (Hirst 2002; da Silva et al 2018) for developing and renewing democracy and the welfare state through greater citizen involvement and a greater role for the third sector.

Cai's involvement in Rhos-based cultural initiatives, such as the Rhos Panto and the Welsh Choir competition, illustrates a similar pattern of local entrepreneurship. In his case, the value to the community lies in Cai's attempt to help Rhos gain recognition within Wales' linguistic and cultural landscape and attract enough funding to preserve landmarks such as the Stiwt and to provide activities such as choirs. The interesting biographical aspect of this case is the reciprocity of Cai's relationship with Rhos. On the one hand, Cai is leveraging his own professional activities to promote Rhos, but at the same time he is using Rhos to enhance his own career pathway. This relationship takes place from a distance, as Cai does not live in Rhos himself.

This type of local entrepreneurship, which links individual economic activities with the process of contributing towards some broader 'value' to the community is an interesting aspect of civil society participation. It highlights the importance of understanding the role of individual norms of civility present in commitments, recognition of community needs and values. Biographical experiences and attachments create an environment in which entrepreneurial individuals are encouraged to align their economic activities with the interest of their wider community. This type of local activity is invaluable for building and expanding civil society at the local level as well as identifying and addressing particular problems and challenges. The analysis of biographies from Rhos and Overton indicates that local entrepreneurs, supported by the wider community, can drive the growth of civil society structures at a local level.

## Economic solidarities

The final analytical link between the local economy and civil society participation points towards economic solidarities as a manifestation of civil society engagement. This particular link is embedded in the forms of charitability, which share both individual and community-based resources with specific people or for specific causes. In this form, participation in civil society actions is backed up by capital donated by members of the community and often reflects the community's state of economic wellbeing. This type of charitable pattern reflects the distribution of wealth within the community, as well as between communities, and the community-based social justice patterns that mobilise participation in the name of a specific social cause. Such economic solidarity is reflected in the spectrum of civil society actions, from individual sponsorships to crowd-funding initiatives. The biographical narratives from Rhos and Overton illustrate well how these economic solidarities can have an impact on individual community members as well as civil society structures at large.

On one side of the spectrum in both Rhos and Overton we observe contributions towards community activities. These contributions are usually proportional to the overall means and abilities, and can include financial support, specific services and volunteering contributions. Individuals and businesses are engaged in local sponsorships or business patronages that are mobilised to contribute towards community causes. But more than that, other forms of contribution are also recognised. In Overton, a pub owner allows community meetings to take place on the premises, utilising its central location. Overton's Real Ale Festival is organised with contributions from local businesses and is aimed at gathering financial resources that support community activities throughout the year and attract people to visit, thereby further supporting local economic activity (Muske and Woods 2004). To illustrate how deeply these economic solidarities can reach within the community we should also consider William's account of community charity during the miners' strikes, when he and his family were without an income for a year. It was other community members, who were themselves not in a good financial situation, who nevertheless contributed directly to his survival by providing food and clothes for him and his children.

Economic solidarities are based on the mobilisation of economic resources, both large and small, to address a specific issue within the community life and so contribute towards the ideal of a good society. It can be found now in crowd-funding initiatives that range from support for local schools and libraries, to assistance for youth groups and people in need, such as food banks. This link between the economic aspect of charity and solidarity and local civil society illustrates how powerful and economically formidable those types of solidarities can be. But understanding the process of economic mobilisation in context, by looking at both Overton and Rhos, draws attention also to the social aspect of economic mobilisation, such as sense of belonging, shared responsibilities, solidarities and norms of civility. Without these social ties, access to individual economic resources is limited and puts any civil society initiatives at the mercy of private capital or state support which often come with a different set of goals and objectives.

## Linking state and institutions to the analysis of civil society participation

Together with the analysis of the economic factors, the nexus between civil society participation and institutions associated with the state in Overton and Rhos also show interesting dynamics. The analysis of structural patterns of participation along lines of age, class and gender, and biographical narratives that relate individuals' participation in civil society activities, points towards the impact of specific policies and programmes on the organisation and support for particular initiatives as well as overlapping leadership structures that combine roles within civil society and local authorities (the County Council in Wrexham as well as community councils in Rhos and Overton). These dynamics have a significant impact on civil society wellbeing, as they have the ability to overwhelm grassroots initiatives and impose external political agendas as well as organisational structures that disrupt the balance of interests and challenge the norms of solidarity and civility. In our empirical data, state interventions feature in most of the civil society actions, and we can identify three main respects in which they impact on civil society.

## The role of policy interventions

State institutions' interventions in civil society structures at the local level are delivered in the various forms of protection policy. These are designed to preserve and support those elements of the local economic and cultural landscape which are identified as valuable for society at large. These policies, state programmes and funding are top-down initiatives that come with a clear political agenda as well as providing economic resources that are particularly coveted by local communities and civil society organisations. Both in Rhos and Overton, we observe some engagement of local civil society in the pursuit of government funding to support the community infrastructure, protect sites of cultural heritage and encourage new revitalising initiatives. But the top-down nature of this type of programme comes with a set of challenges. State interventions require specific policy alignment, forcing civil society initiatives to be framed in terms of objectives as well as structures along the lines of current political agendas that deem some initiatives worthy and others unworthy of recognition and support. Such interventions can create 'protection bubbles' which, in the long term, lead to state institutions overpowering local civil society and encasing local civil society structures within state structures.

Yet many of the activities found in the localities are organic. They differ from centralised state initiatives or market forces in that they identify and utilise the strengths existing within localities to create more sustainable communities. The Overton Playgroup, the Beer Festival and in Rhos the ongoing campaign to keep the Stiwt open are all examples of such activity. The much-overused phrase 'bottom-up' is appropriate here, as local people deploy existing, rather than assigned or devolved assets from elsewhere. As can be observed in both sites of study, such community assets can be individual, associational, cultural or environmental, as well as economic (Russell 2021). Their success, however, can be related to the availability of community assets and the leverage this affords. Community assets are inherently spread unequally, leaving some places particularly vulnerable when external market or state protection is required or relied upon.

## Policy protectionism

'Protection bubbles' are a particularly prominent feature in Rhos' civil society initiatives. Rhos was built on the mining industry which was prioritised and protected in the post-war economy when the whole coal industry was nationalised. The collapse of mining is an example of what the withdrawal of protection can do to an economic sector, leaving communities and people without employment opportunities and straining local support networks. William's story especially shows how the cherished way of life can disappear within a year when state institutions withdraw their support. But this is not the only 'protection bubble' that made Rhos particularly dependent on state interventions. Its celebrated mining past has left the village with a number of heritage objects, such as the remnants of the mines themselves and the Stiwt. These sites require an increasing amount of capital to run and preserve, which is beyond the reach of local civil society institutions and makes them dependent on changeable state support. To secure this line of funding, the community's focus is fixated on the procedures and objectives as well as business cases that come to redefine their role in the community just in order to meet the latest policy agenda. This steers away from civil society's role in creating value for the community at large. The outcome is a sense of survival, yet another disaster avoided, with a noticeable lack of energy and vision for the future.

In this context, even the relatively successful actions of Cai and his attempts to restore Rhos' unique cultural importance in Wales' cultural landscape can be seen as part of a similar 'protective bubble'. The Welsh Language Board was created to support the minority language in social institutions, including the media, education and public service. They provide resources as well as media outlets that enable the creation and distribution of new cultural content. However, the reach of this content is limited to other Welsh-speaking consumers. Rhos' Panto was broadcast on S4C television with English subtitles, but its impact beyond that medium and that audience was very limited, not only because of the language, but also the lack of means that would take a particular cultural product beyond simple preservation and into promotion mode.

Civil society participation is significantly impacted by state institution programmes that contribute to the emergence of 'protective bubbles'. By overwhelming the local structures with resources fitted to specific political agendas, they redirect the energy and attention within communities, with little regard to their particular strengths. Those objects and practices that are protected thrive for some time, expanding activity and recruiting members. Inevitably, however, when resources are withdrawn, these types of initiatives and programmes tend to fail. This is due to a lack of grass-root support that is built over time and embedded in individual solidarities and the creation of overblown, unsustainable infrastructures that, as in the case of Rhos' Miner's Institute, ultimately become a drain on the already limited community resources.

## Policy alignment

In contrast to Rhos, Overton seems to have avoided most of the threats associated with 'economic bubbles' with a wider breadth and depth of community strength and assets to draw upon. In the biographical narratives we can find a different type of link between state institutions and civil society participation, which can be referred to as policy alignment. This practice is associated with the patterns of local entrepreneurship discussed within the section on the economy. In the cases of both Karen and Susan, there is an element of local initiatives, such as attempts to tackle littering or organise a childminding network, that originated from individual action within the local civil society and were successful enough to be picked up by the local authorities and councils as they aligned with the policy priorities at the given time. For example, environmental policies can be used to support activities such as litter collections or wildlife maintenance to a certain extent, but usually with minimal resources. The same is the case with services such as childminding which, due to licencing regulations, are connected to local council structures but need an extended servicing, such as access to information networks, to be used by the community.

The type of civil society action that aligns successfully with policy priorities can tap into limited resources at council and government level and often depends on volunteers to carry out the main part of activities. This collaborative effort seems less disruptive than grander protection policies, towards civil society organisation. Because it depends on volunteers, there is an interest in building and maintaining the local solidarities and norms of civility that would attract people who want to participate in civil society actions. This policy support, however, depends on the most current understanding of priorities, which tend to change according to shifts in the broader political landscapes and current debates. Changes in direction of local funding as well as the complex procedures of applying and executing those funds require skills and resources that become an operational capital within the community, linking this point back to the discussion on local entrepreneurship and the broader patterns of class, gender, age and place.

## Co-opting local leadership

The final point on the relations between civil society participation and state institutions is the overlap of council structures with local leadership structures, which can be observed in both sites. Susan's case from Overton is particularly relevant. Her initiative to pick up litter was well aligned with the environmental priorities, and as the initiative tapped into the resources and support available at the council level, it put Susan in a unique situation of leadership, which was later on recognised at the community level, where she engaged in a number of other clubs and activities. In that position, running for community councillor was a natural progression of her leadership role. She embraced the transition from what was a volunteer civil society structure into a paid position. In this transition, there is a subtle difference in priorities and responsibilities which, in some cases, may lead to a dissonance between the interests of the community and the job requirements of councillors. In her role as a community councillor, Susan is expected to follow an administrative procedure, such as consultation process, to channel resistance within the civil society into an administrative process. What could be an act of open resistance, here is directed into the 'dialogue' with the state institution, which may or may not admit the civil society voice into consideration. While this process works relatively well for Overton, at least for now, since the development proposal has been suspended, potentially it may also act to overrule the position expressed by civil society.

## Conclusion

The analysis of civil society participation patterns and the links between the local economy and the state institutions highlights an intricate network of relationships. The focus on the interactions between economic resources and the impact of government policies indicates that civil society actions should be investigated as part of an ecosystem which exists in a balance of power relations between the interest of individuals, the community and the broader socio-political and economic context. Civil society participation in both Rhos and Overton is embedded in the ties of solidarity and civility built and reinforced by long-term, biographical attachments. The analysis of diverse civil society actions and the ways in which they have been embedded in the narratives indicates tensions between the concept of the good life from the perspective of the individual and local community and from the perspective of political institutions and economic relations. We explored these tensions by examining the links between the economy, state institutions and civil society participation accounts from Rhos and Overton.

In this chapter we have argued that links between civil society participation and the economy are crucial for understanding the role of civil society actions within the context of local communities. Civil society actions constitute the first line of response to economic threats; they provide protection of individual community members and build synergies between economic activities and civil society participation. Firstly, we observed that civil society aims to counter wider shifts in the economy at large. The disruption in the economic base, either in terms of withdrawal of capital, such as the closure of a local employer, or influx, such as new development initiatives, is met with a civil society response that aims to resist changes and restore economic equilibrium. Secondly, economic solidarities that mobilise the collective economic base, such as crowd-funding or local sponsorship, are used to financially support an initiative and individuals at moments of financial hardship. Finally, participation in civil society activities can activate and support local entrepreneurs who, through economic activities, deliver additional value to their local communities, such as building a valuable service or providing a platform for further civil society actions.

# Conclusion

Throughout this book we have emphasised the fundamental importance of both place and time to civil society and its operation across varied local socio-spatial contexts. By concentrating on two localities within the same frame of reference, we have been able to demonstrate how a sense of difference is constructed. While we have tried to avoid treating these places as fixed and bounded, we nevertheless observe how most people's participation remains rooted and locally orientated, challenging the notion that local civil society is inevitably being hollowed-out by the global. Indeed, the overriding message of our work is the extent to which sustainability of local civil society in these two contexts rests upon lifelong and deeply held attachments to place. We conclude by summarising both the scholarly and policy significance of this analysis.

To begin with, the account of civil society we have provided goes far beyond the prevailing notions of volunteering, voluntary associations and third sector organisations – notions which dominate the policy and governmental understanding of civil society. Instead we have used the framework of local civil society in order to document a much broader material and symbolic sphere of situated forms of association, civility, participation and solidarity. Such a broad terrain, we have argued, cannot be adequately understood without reference to its localised setting or indeed to its biographical significance for individuals.

In exploring how the local world of civil society is sustained, we have focused on the lives of individuals who display strong emotional attachments to the places in which they live, and who invest considerable time and effort in establishing and supporting local groups and shared activities. Our biographical data highlights the importance within people's life stories of action at the local level: doing things with and for the people they live among, and with whom they can identify; protecting and improving the place they inhabit, including maintaining its 'heritage'; and receiving and passing on between generations the accumulated legacy of their community, according to their understanding of its value and purpose. Whether their roots were 'local' to begin with, or they arrived on the scene later in life, these were individuals who entered the field primed for local involvement. Their active engagement with and participation in civil society was empowered and directed by individual experiences collected and nurtured over considerable stretches of time, which also enabled them to make connections between the very concrete concerns of everyday life at local level and some of the more general and abstract themes of citizenship, civility and solidarity. The life of local associations synchronised with the embodied attachments which these actors had built and sustained over their lifetime. We also noted that individuals with international experiences and connections were able to add a further layer to civil society operations, by building new networks and introducing new ideas.

Hence, with the use of biographical methods and a focus on narratives of place and time, we have tried to make visible the connection between civil society, social self-organising and the symbolic landscapes of belonging. This is not only a matter of biographical availability – the time and labour resources of individuals – but also of the way in which the civility or incivility of local life is itself a temporal question. Whereas in some contexts, civility arises from the opportunities for spontaneous interactions between diverse others, in other contexts its accomplishment is dependent upon the extended time frame needed to work through complex local problems and put in place the networks which enable trust and maintain cooperation – the dimension of community time. The obvious policy implication of this latter point is how easily the short-term, time-limited, support offered through place-based funding schemes, and tied to changing political agendas, comes into conflict with the extended time period required to formulate and address community problems. In their accounts of grappling with these issues actors raised concerns about the future renewal of local civil society and dilemmas of succession. In their narratives we found a significant element of nostalgia, relating to their sense of time, and the maintenance of continuity.

Returning to the themes of the early chapters, our analysis presents some questions for theories of civil society, many of which seek to establish, explicitly or implicitly, a marked distance from local particularistic communities and identities. While to some extent the distinction between community and association has been superseded, it is still a theme which continues to have resonance within current sociological and geographical debates around the local and the cosmopolitan, conviviality, local progressivism, and their specific delineations of civil and uncivil kinds of social relations. This poses a question which is highly relevant for our approach, as to whether a clear line can be drawn between studying local civil society and studying community. Making assessments about the changing nature of local civil society requires familiarity with the broad and diverse body of local research previously undertaken. By locating our own fieldwork, and other recent studies, within the wider scholarship on civil society as well as local communities, we suggest that there is much more continuity between the recent attention given to convivial and progressive forms of local life and the recognition of differences found in older community studies than is often credited. We have acknowledged previous contributions which challenge overly negative interpretations of community studies, and indeed seek to counter those theoretical arguments which bring into question the very concept of community, as well as local empirical studies which refute the over-theorised opposition between the local and cosmopolitan. Current research on local constructions of conviviality has also emphasised the need to account for its co-existence with everyday forms of closure, exclusion and racism. An overall lesson we take from these different endeavours is the need for local studies which are sensitised, firstly, to teasing out equally both the civil and the uncivil dimensions of community life, and, secondly, to an awareness that there is no simple correspondence between local civil society and the local versus cosmopolitan, regressive or progressive, distinction.

Finally, our analysis also indicates that highly focused political agendas can lead to the creation of 'protective bubbles' within communities. Existing research has already noted the tendency of policy priorities and the delivery modes of development and regeneration programmes to disrupt the power balance between state and local civil society, frequently leading to state-dependency and the risk of failure when support is withdrawn. Selective place-based funding has often been based on a deficit model that identifies key 'problems' in communities such as high unemployment or poor housing or a perceived lack of social capital. These problems are often too large for communities to tackle on their own but the policy imperative can overshadow and stifle other civil society priorities and actions. In our findings, we observed a tendency for state institutions to overtake and incorporate local civil society leadership structures. While this process eases the communication and administrative links between communities and local authorities, it can sometimes lead to problems when the interests of an authority and the community come into conflict, bringing a sense that local actors have been stripped of control, or had their voices silenced. On the other hand, of course, bottom-up initiatives, such as asset-based community development or local entrepreneurship, can benefit from state support but require a light-touch and readiness to cede control that state institutions inevitably find challenging. Civil society initiatives that can be aligned with current policy priorities can tap into resources which can be used to develop a local service or invest in infrastructure and thus benefit the community. Our findings highlight the role and value of local civil society actors, and the importance of recognising their insights, in order to strike a balance between policy priorities and bottom-up initiatives.

# Notes

## Chapter 3

1. *Papurau Bro* (plural) are Welsh-language local community newsletters, produced by volunteers and generally published monthly. Most receive funding from the Welsh Government to promote Welsh language in local communities.
2. The publication in 1847 of the three-volume Reports of the Commissioners of Enquiry into the State of Education in Wales – known as the Blue Books – is now widely interpreted as the judgements of an English bourgeoisie on a language they could not speak, a literature they deemed unworthy and forms of culture and worship they either could not understand or mistrusted (Fitz 2001).
3. There are notable exceptions such as Poundbury (Thompson-Fawcett 2003) in Dorset which continues a long tradition of model estate developments.
4. The ACORN dataset analyses significant social factors and population behaviour, providing information and in-depth understanding of the different types of people. See https://acorn.caci.co.uk/
5. The Aelwyd is a branch of the Urdd organisation – the Welsh League of Youth.
6. Band of Hope was a chapel-based temperance youth group.

# References

Abram, S. (1998) 'Class, countryside and the "longitudinal study": a response to Hoggart', *Journal of Rural Studies*, 14(3): 369–79.

Abrams, P. (1972) 'The sense of the past and the origins of sociology', *Past & Present*, 55: 18–32.

Adam, B. (1990) *Time and Social Theory*, Cambridge: Polity Press.

Agnew, J.A. (1987) *Place and Politics: The Geographical Mediation of State and Society*, London: Allen and Unwin.

Alexander, J.C. (1997) 'The paradoxes of civil society', *International Sociology*, 12(2): 115–33.

Alexander, J.C. (1998) 'Constructing an empirical concept from normative controversies and historical transformation', in J.C. Alexander (ed) *Real Civil Societies: The Dilemma of Institutionalization*, London: Sage, pp 1–19.

Alexander, J.C. (2006) *The Civil Sphere*, Oxford: Oxford University Press.

Amin, A. (2004) 'Regions unbound: towards a new politics of place', *Geografiska Annaler. Series B, Human Geography*, 86(1): 33–44.

Amin, A. (2005) 'Local community on trial', *Economy and Society*, 34(4): 612–33.

Amit, V. and Rapport, N. (2002) *The Trouble with Community: Anthropological Reflections on Movement, Identity and Collectivity*, London: Pluto Press.

Anderson, B. (1991) *Imagined Communities* (revised edition), London: Verso.

Ashmore, R.D., Deaux, K. and McLaughlin-Volpe, T. (2004) 'An organizing framework for collective identity: articulation and significance of multidimensionality', *Psychological Bulletin*, 130(1): 80–114.

Back, L. (2009) 'Researching community and its moral projects', *Twenty-First Century Society*, 4(2): 201–14.

Barrett, G. (2015) 'Deconstructing community', *Sociologia Ruralis*, 55(2): 182–204.

Baumgarten, B., Gosewinkel, D. and Rucht, D. (2011) 'Civility: introductory notes on the history and systematic analysis of a concept', *European Review of History*, 18(3): 289–312.

BBC (2019) 'Rhosllanerchrugog's Stiwt clock chimes after decade of silence'. Available at: www.bbc.co.uk/news/uk-wales-48226496

Bell, C. (1968) *Middle Class Families: Social and Geographical Mobility*, London: Routledge.

Bell, C. and Newby, H. (1971) *Community Studies: An Introduction to the Local Community*, London: Allen & Unwin.

Bell, C. and Newby, H. (1976) 'Community, communion, class and community action: the social sources of the new urban politics', in D.J. Herbert and R.J. Johnson (eds) *Social Areas in Cities*, Chichester: John Wiley, pp 189–207.

Bell, M.M. (1994) *Childerley: Nature and Morality in a Country Village*, Chicago: University of Chicago Press.

Bennett, J. (2018) 'Narrating family histories: negotiating identity and belonging through tropes of nostalgia and authenticity', *Current Sociology*, 66(3): 449–65.

Benson, M. and Jackson, E. (2013) 'Place-making and place maintenance: performativity, place and belonging among the middle classes', *Sociology*, 47(4): 793–809.

Berger, P.L. and Luckmann, T. (1966) *The Social Construction of Reality*, New York: Anchor.

Berman, S. (1997) 'Civil society and the collapse of the Weimar Republic', *World Politics*, 49(3): 401–29.

Best, E. and Pike, B. (eds) (1948) *International Voluntary Service for Peace 1920–1946*, London: George Allen and Unwin.

Blokland, T. (2001) 'Bricks, mortar, memories: neighbourhood and networks in collective acts of remembering', *International Journal of Urban and Regional Research*, 25(2): 268–83.

Blythe, R. (1969) *Akenfield: Portrait of an English Village*, Harmondsworth: Penguin.

Born, B. and Purcell, M. (2006) 'Avoiding the local trap: scale and food systems in planning research', *Journal of Planning Education and Research*, 26(2): 195–207.

Boyle, P. and Halfacree, K. (eds) (1998) *Migration into Rural Areas*, Chichester: John Wiley.

Brehm, J.M., Eisenhauer, B.W. and Krannich, R.S. (2006) 'Community attachments as predictors of local environmental concern', *American Behavioral Scientist*, 50(2): 142–65.

Bruce, S. (2010) 'Religion in rural Wales: four restudies', *Contemporary Wales*, 23(1): 219–39.

Buchowski, M. (1996) 'The shifting meanings of civil and civic Society in Poland', in C. Hann and E. Dunn (eds) *Civil Society: Challenging Western Models*, London: Routledge, pp 79–98.

Bulmer, M. (1986) *Neighbours: The Work of Philip Abrams*, Cambridge: Cambridge University Press.

Cabinet Office (2015) *Community Life Survey Statistical Bulletin*. Available at: https://assets.publishing.service.gov.uk/government/uploads/system/uploads/attachment_data/file/539102/2015_16_community_life_survey_bulletin_final.pdf

Calhoun, C. (2003) '"Belonging" in the cosmopolitan imaginary', *Ethnicities*, 3(4): 531–53.

Calhoun, C. (2007) *Nations Matter: Culture, History and the Cosmopolitan Dream*, London: Routledge.

Calhoun, C. (2011) 'Civil society and the public sphere', in M. Edwards, (ed) *The Oxford Handbook of Civil Society*, New York: Oxford University Press, pp 311–23.

Cameron, D. (2010) Big Society Speech. Available at: www.number10.gov.uk/news/big-society-speech/

Cameron, H. (2001) 'Social capital in Britain: are Hall's membership figures a reliable guide?', *Unpublished paper presented at the ARNOVA Conference*, Miami, FL.

Carter, H. (1996) 'Foreword' to reissue of A.D. Rees, *Life in a Welsh Countryside*, Cardiff: University of Wales Press, pp 1–10.

Castells, M. (2008) 'The new public sphere: global civil society, communication networks, and global governance', *The Annals of the American Academy of Political and Social Science*, 616(1): 78–93.

Chambers, S. (2002) 'A critical theory of civil society' in S. Chambers and W. Kymlicka (eds) *Alternative Conceptions of Civil Society*, Princeton: Princeton University Press, pp 90–110.

Charles, N. and Davies, C.A. (2005) 'Studying the particular, illuminating the general: community studies and community in Wales', *The Sociological Review*, 53(4): 672–90.

Cloke, P., Goodwin, M. and Milbourne, P. (1997) *Rural Wales: Community and Marginalization*, Cardiff: University of Wales Press.

Clwyd Powys Archaeological Trust (n.d.) *Historic Settlement Survey*, Overton: Wrexham County Borough.

Cnaan, R.A., Handy, F. and Wadsworth, M. (1996) 'Defining who is a volunteer: conceptual and empirical considerations', *Nonprofit and Voluntary Sector Quarterly*, 25(3): 364–83.

Coflein (2020) *Overton on Dee* (online catalogue of archaeology, buildings, industrial and maritime heritage in Wales). Available at: https://coflein.gov.uk/en

Cohen, A. (1982) *Belonging: Identity and Social Organisation in British Rural Cultures*, Manchester: Manchester University Press.

Cohen, A. (1985) *The Symbolic Construction of Community*, London: Routledge.

Cohen, A. (2005) 'Village on the border, anthropology at the crossroads: the significance of a classic British ethnography', *Sociological Review*, 53(4): 603–20.

Cohen, J.L. (2007) 'Civil society and globalization: rethinking the categories', in L. Tragardh (ed) *State and Civil Society in Northern Europe: The Swedish Model Reconsidered*, Oxford: Berghahn Books, pp 37–66.

Cohen, J.L. and Arato, A. (1992) *Civil Society and Political Theory*, Cambridge, MA: MIT Press.

Cohen, P. (1997) 'Beyond the community romance', *Soundings*, 5: 29–51.

Cornwall, A. (2002) 'Making spaces, changing spaces: situating participation in development', *IDS Paper* 170, Falmer: University of Sussex.

Crehan, K. (2002) *Gramsci, Culture and Anthropology*, Berkeley: University of California Press.

Crehan, K. (2006) 'Hunting the unicorn: art and community in East London', in G.W. Creed (ed) *The Seductions of Community: Emancipations, Oppressions, Quandaries*, Santa Fe: SAR Press, pp 49–76.

Cresswell, T. (2009) 'Place' in *International Encyclopedia of Human Geography*, 8, 169–77.

Crow, G. (2008) 'Recent rural community studies', *International Journal of Social Research Methodology*, 11(2): 131–39.

Crow, G. and Allan, G. (1994) *Community Life: An Introduction to Local Social Relations*, London: Harvester Wheatsheaf.

Crow, G. and Takeda, N. (2011) 'Ray Pahl's sociological career: fifty years of impact', *Sociological Research Online*, 16(3): 184–93.

Dallimore, D. (2016) 'A neoliberal inconvenience', WISERD Blog. Available at: https://wiserd.ac.uk/news/neoliberal-

Dallimore, D.J., Davis, H., Eichsteller, M. and Mann, R. (2018) 'Place, belonging and the determinants of volunteering', *Voluntary Sector Review*, 9(1): 21–38.

da Silva, D.S., Horlings, L.G. and Figueiredo, E. (2018) 'Citizen initiatives in the post-welfare state', *Social Sciences*, 7(12): 252–73.

Davies, J. (2007) *A History of Wales*, Cardiff: University of Wales Press.

Davies, E. and Rees, A.D. (eds) (1960) *Welsh Rural Communities*, Cardiff: University of Wales Press.

Davis. H., Dallimore, D., Eichsteller, M. and Mann, R. (2021) 'Religion and local civil society', *Journal of Contemporary Religion*. Available at: https://www.tandfonline.com/doi/full/10.1080/13537903.2021.1936967

Dawson, M.T.C. and Bhatt, M.G. (2001) 'The IMF and civil society: striking a balance', *Policy Discussion Paper* (No. 01/2), Washington: International Monetary Fund.

Day, G. (1998a) 'Working with the grain? Towards sustainable rural and community development', *Journal of Rural Studies*, 14(1): 89–105.

Day, G. (1998b) 'A community of communities? Similarity and difference in Welsh rural community studies', *Economic and Social Review*, 29(3): 233–57.

Day, G. (2006a) 'Civil society and rural Wales', in G. Day, D. Dunkerley and A. Thompson (eds) *Civil Society in Wales: Policy, Politics and People*, Cardiff: University of Wales Press, pp 227–45.

Day, G. (2006b) *Community and Everyday Life*, London: Routledge.

Day, G. and Murdoch, J. (1993) 'Locality and community: coming to terms with place', *The Sociological Review*, 41(1): 82–111.

Dench, G., Gavron, K. and Young, M. (2006) *The New East End: Kinship, Race and Conflict*, London: Profile Books.

Dennis, N., Henriques, F. and Slaughter, C. (1956) *Coal Is Our Life*, London: Eyre and Spottiswoode.

Diani, M. (2005) 'Cities in the world: local civil society and global issues in Britain', in D. Della Porta and S. Tarrow (eds) *Transnational Protest and Global Activism*, Lanham: Rowman and Littlefield, pp 45–67.

Dodd, A.H. (1971) *The Industrial Revolution in North Wales*, Cardiff: University of Wales Press.

Done, B. and Williams, B. (1992) *Overton in Times Past. A Brief History*, Mold: Cwyd County Council.

Durkheim, E. (1893/1964) *The Division of Labour in Society*, Glencoe: Free Press.

Edmondson, R. (2000) 'Rural temporal practices: future time in Connemara', *Time and Society*, 9(2–3): 269–88.

Edwards, M. (2014) *Civil Society* (3rd edn), Cambridge: Polity.

Elias, N. (1987) 'The retreat of sociologists into the present', *Theory, Culture & Society*, 4(2–3): 223–47.

Elias, N. and Scotson, J. (1965) *The Established and the Outsiders: A Sociological Enquiry into Community Problems*, London: Frank Cass & Co Ltd.

Ellis, K. and Bolton, P. (2016) *A 'Mansion for Miners': Plas Mwynwyr, Rhosllannerchrugog*, Cardiff: Rowanvale Books.

Emmett, I. (1964) *A North Wales Village: A Social Anthropological Study*, London: Routledge & Kegan Paul.

Evers, A. (2010) 'Observations on incivility: blind spots in third sector research and policy', *Voluntary Sector Review*, 1(1): 113–17.

Falk, R. (1998) 'Global civil society: perspectives, initiatives, movements', *Oxford Development Studies*, 26 (1): 99–110.

Ferguson, A. (1980) *An Essay on the History of Civil Society, 1767*, London: Transaction Publishers.

Fitz, J. (2001) 'Local identity and national systems: the case of Wales', in N.K. Shimahara, I.Z. Holowinsky and S. Tomlinson-Clarke (eds) *Ethnicity, Race, and Nationality in Education: A Global Perspective*, London: Routledge, pp 233–58.

Flaherty, M.G. and Fine, G.A. (2001) 'Present, past, and future', *Time and Society*, 10(2–3): 147–61.

Frankenberg, R. (1957) *Village on the Border: A Social Study of Religion, Politics and Football in a North Wales Community*, Manchester: Manchester University Press.

Frankenberg, R. (1969) *Communities in Britain*, Harmondsworth: Penguin.

Gans, H. (1968) 'Urbanisation and suburbanism as ways of life', in H. Gans (ed) *People and Plans: Essays on Urban Problems and Solutions*, New York: Basic Books, pp 35–52.

Gans, H.J. (1992) 'Sociological amnesia: the noncumulation of normal social science', *Sociological Forum*, 7(4): 701–10.

Georgiou, M. (2017) 'Conviviality is not enough: a communication perspective to the city of difference', *Communication, Culture & Critique*, 10(2): 261–79.

Georgiou, M. (2020) 'Solidarity at the time of COVID-19: an(other) digital revolution?', *LSE Blog*, 30 March 2020. Available at: https://blogs.lse.ac.uk/medialse/2020/03/30/solidarity-at-the-time-of-covid-19-another-digital-revolution/

Gilroy, P. (2004) *After Empire: Melancholia or Convivial Culture?*, London: Routledge.

Gøtzsche-Astrup, J. (2019) 'Civil society and its outside: analysing the boundary between civil and uncivil society in the Danish anti-radicalization discourse', *Journal of Civil Society*, 15(2): 162–77.

Green Flag Award 'Raising the standard of Parks and Green Spaces'. Available at: www.greenflagaward.org/park-summary/?ParkID=1166

Grenier, P. and Wright, K. (2006) 'Social capital in Britain: exploring the Hall Paradox', *Policy Studies*, 27(1): 27–53.

Guma, T., Woods, M., Yarker, S. and Anderson, J. (2019) '"It's that kind of place here": solidarity, place-making and civil society response to the 2015 refugee crisis in Wales, UK', *Social Inclusion*, 7(2): 96–105.

Gustafson, P. (2014) 'Place attachment in an age of mobility', in L.C. Manzo and P. Devine-Wright (eds) *Place Attachment: Advances in Theory, Methods and Applications*, New York: Routledge, pp 37–48.

Habermas, J. (1996) *Between Facts and Norms: Contributions to a Discourse Theory of Law and Democracy*, Cambridge, MA: MIT Press.

Hall, P.A. (1999) 'Social capital in Britain', *British Journal of Political Science*, 29(3): 417–61.

Halpern, D. (2005) *Social Capital*, Cambridge: Polity Press.

Hambleton, R. (2020) *Cities and Communities Beyond Covid-19*, Bristol: Bristol University Press.

Han, J. (2017) 'Social marketisation and policy influence of third sector organisations: evidence from the UK', *Voluntas: International Journal of Voluntary and Nonprofit Organisations*, 28: 1209–25.

Hancock, L., Mooney, G. and Neal, S. (2012) 'Crisis social policy and the resilience of the concept of community', *Critical Social Policy*, 32(3): 343–64.

Hann, C. (1992) 'Civil society at the grass-roots: a reactionary view', in P.G. Lewis (ed) *Democracy and Civil Society in Eastern Europe*, London: Palgrave Macmillan, pp 152–65.

Hann, C. (1996) 'Introduction: political society and civil anthropology', in C. Hann and E. Dunn (eds) *Civil Society: Challenging Western Models*, London: Routledge, pp 1–26.

Harper, S. (1989) 'The British rural community: an overview of perspectives', *Journal of Rural Studies*, 5(2): 161–84.

Harvey, D. (1989) *The Condition of Postmodernity*, Oxford: Blackwell.

Harvey, D. (1996) *Justice, Nature and the Geography of Difference*, Cambridge, MA: Blackwell.

Heley, J. and Jones, L. (2012) 'Relational rurals: some thoughts on relating things and theory in rural studies', *Journal of Rural Studies*, 28(3): 208–17.

Heritage Lottery Fund (HLF) (n.d.) The Regeneration of Ponciau Banks Park. Available at: www.lotterygoodcauses.org.uk/project/regeneration-ponciau-banks-park

Hirst, P. (2002) 'Renewing democracy through associations', *Political Quarterly*, 73(4): 409–21.

Hobbes, T. (1651/1984) *De Cive: The English Version*, Clarendon edition, H. Warrender (ed), Oxford: Oxford University Press.

Hobsbawm, E.J. (1962) *The Age of Revolution 1789–1848*, London: Weidenfeld and Nicolson.

Hoggett, P. (ed) (1997) *Contested Communities: Experiences, Struggles, Policies*, Bristol: Bristol University Press.

Hughes, G. (2008) '"Arwyr lleol" (that's Welsh for local heroes)', *British Journalism Review*, 19(2): 52–7.

Ingen, R.R.W., Symons, J.C. and Johnson, H.V. (1848) *Reports of the Commissioners of Inquiry into the State of Education in Wales: Appointed by the Committee of Council on Education*, Part 3, London: HMSO.

Jackson, A.J.H. (2012) 'The "openclosed" settlement model and the interdisciplinary formulations of Dennis Mills: conceptualising local rural change', *Rural History*, 23(2): 121–36.

Jackson, B. (1968) *Working Class Community: Some General Notions Raised by a Series of Studies in Northern England*, London: Routledge.

Jenkins, D. (1971) *The Agricultural Community in South-west Wales at the Turn of the Twentieth Century*, Cardiff: University of Wales Press.

Jessop, B. (2020) *Putting Civil Society in Its Place: Governance, Metagovernance and Subjectivity*, Bristol: Policy Press.

Jones, L. and Heley, J. (2016) 'Practices of participation and voluntarism among older people in rural Wales: choice, obligation and constraints to active ageing', *Sociologia Ruralis*, 56(2): 176–96.

Kaldor, M. (2003) 'The idea of global civil society', *International Affairs*, 79(3): 583–93.

Keane, J. (1988) *Civil Society and the State: New European Perspectives*, London: University of Westminster Press.

Keane, J. (2009) 'Civil society, definitions and approaches', in H. Anheier and S. Toepler (eds) *International Encyclopedia of Civil Society*, New York: Springer, pp 461–4.

Kisby, B. (2010) 'The Big Society: power to the people?', *The Political Quarterly*, 81(4): 484–91.

Laidlaw, R. (1995) *Community, Work and Religion: Mentalities in the Villages of the North Wales Coalfield c.1930–c.1960*, PhD thesis, University of Warwick.

Lancee, B. and Radl, J. (2014) 'Volunteering over the life course', *Social Forces*, 93(2): 833–62.

Levitas, R. (2004) 'Let's hear it for Humpty: social exclusion, the third way and cultural capital', *Cultural Trends*, 13(2): 41–56.

Levitas, R. (2012) 'The just's umbrella: austerity and the Big Society in coalition policy and beyond', *Critical Social Policy*, 32(3): 320–42.

Lewicka, M. (2005) 'Ways to make people active: the role of place attachment, cultural capital, and neighbourhood ties', *Journal of Environmental Psychology*, 25(4): 381–95.

Lewicka, M. (2008) 'Place attachment, place identity, and place memory: restoring the forgotten city past', *Journal of Environmental Psychology*, 28(3): 209–31.

Lewis, D. (2002) 'Civil society in African contexts: reflections on the usefulness of a concept', *Development and Change*, 33(4): 569–86.

Lewis, G.J. (1986) 'Welsh rural communities: retrospect and prospect', *Cambria*, 13: 27–37.

Lewis, J. (1999) 'Reviewing the relationship between the voluntary sector and the state in Britain in the 1990s', *Voluntas: International Journal of Voluntary and Nonprofit Organisations*, 10(3): 225–70.

Li, Y., Pickles, A. and Savage, M. (2005) 'Social capital and social trust in Britain', *European Sociological Review*, 27(2):109–23.

Liepins, R. (2000) 'New energies for an old idea: reworking approaches to community in contemporary rural studies', *Journal of Rural Studies*, 16(1): 23–35.

Littlejohn, J. (1963) *Westrigg: The Sociology of a Cheviot Parish*, London: Routledge.

Lofland, L.H. (1989) 'Social life in the public realm: a review', *Journal of Contemporary Ethnography*, 17(4): 453–82.

Low, S.M. and Altman, I. (1992) 'Place attachment: a conceptual inquiry', in I. Altman and S.M. Low (eds) *Place Attachment*, New York: Plenum Press, pp 1–12.

Lynch, K. (1960) *The Image of The City*, Cambridge, MA: MIT Press.

Lynch, K. (1972) *What Time is The Place*, Cambridge, MA: MIT Press.

Mann, M. (1973) *Workers on the Move*, Cambridge: Cambridge University Press.

Mann, R. and Fenton, S. (2017) *Nation, Class and Resentment: The Politics of National Identity in England, Scotland and Wales*, London: Palgrave Macmillan.

Marshall, T.F. (1997) *Local Voluntary Activity Surveys (LOVAS): Research Manual*, London: Home Office Research and Statistics Directorate.

Massey, D. (1991a) 'A global sense of place', *Marxism Today*, 38: 24–9.

Massey, D. (1991b) 'The political place of locality studies', *Environment and Planning A*, 23(2): 267–81.

Massey, D. (2005) *For Space*, London: Sage.

McBeath, G. and Webb, S. (1997) 'Cities, subjectivity and cyberspace', in S. Westwood and J. Williams (eds) *Imagining Cities: Scripts, Signs, Memory*, London: Routledge, pp 249–60.

McCabe, A. and Phillimore, J. (2009) 'Exploring below the radar: issues of theme and focus', *Third Sector Research Centre, Briefing Paper No. 8*, University of Birmingham.

McCabe, A. and Phillimore, J. (eds) (2018) *Community Groups in Context: Local Activities and Actions*, Bristol: Policy Press.

McCabe, A., Phillimore, J. and Mayblin, L. (2010) 'Below the radar' activities and organisations in the third sector: a summary review of the literature', *Third Sector Research Centre, Working Paper 29*, University of Birmingham.

McCulloch, A. (2014) 'Cohort variations in the membership of voluntary associations in Great Britain, 1991–2007', *Sociology*, 48(1): 167–85.

McFarlane, C. (2009) 'Translocal assemblages: space, power and social movements', *Geoforum*, 40(4): 561–7.

McIlwaine, C. (2007) 'From local to global to transnational civil society: reframing development perspectives on the non-state sector', *Geography Compass*, 1(6): 1252–81.

Mead, G. H. (1934) *Mind, Self and Society*, Chicago: University of Chicago Press.

Meyer, M. and Hyde, C. (2004) 'Too much of a "good" thing? Insular neighbourhood associations, nonreciprocal civility, and the promotion of civic health', *Nonprofit and Voluntary Sector Quarterly*, 33(3_supp): 77–96.

Milbourne, P. and Kitchen, L. (2014) 'Rural mobilities: connecting movement and fixity in rural places', *Journal of Rural Studies*, 34: 326–36.

Milligan, C. and Fyfe, N.R. (2004) 'Putting the voluntary sector in its place: geographical perspectives on voluntary activity and social welfare in Glasgow', *Journal of Social Policy*, 33(1): 73–93.

Mills, D.R. (1973) 'The development of rural settlement around Lincoln', in D.R. Mills (ed) *English Rural Communities*, London: Macmillan, pp 83–97.

Mohan, G. and Mohan, J. (2002) 'Placing social capital', *Progress in Human Geography*, 26(2): 191–210.

Mooney, G. and Fyfe, N. (2006) 'New labour and community protests: the case of the Govanhill swimming pool campaign, Glasgow', *Local Economy*, 21(2): 136–50.

Moore, R. (2008) '"Careless talk": a critique of Dench, Gavron and Young's *The New East End*', *Critical Social Policy*, 28(3): 349–60.

Murdoch, J. and Marsden, T. (1994) *Reconstituting Rurality: Class, Community and Power in the Development Process*, London: UCL Press.

Muske, G. and Woods, M. (2004) 'Micro businesses as an economic development tool: what they bring and what they need', *Community Development Society Journal*, 35(1): 97–116.

Neal, S. (2016) *Rural Identities: Ethnicity and Community in the Contemporary English Countryside*, London: Routledge.

Neal, S., Bennett, K., Cochrane, A. and Mohan, G. (2019) 'Community and conviviality? Informal social life in multicultural places', *Sociology*, 53(1): 69–86.

Newby, H. (1980) *Green and Pleasant Land? Social Change in Rural England*, Harmondsworth: Penguin.

Nowicka, M. (2020) 'Fantasy of conviviality: banalities of multicultural settings and what we do (not) notice when we look at them', in O. Hemer, M. Povrzanović Frykman and P.M. Ristilammi (eds) *Conviviality at the Crossroads: The Poetics and Politics of Everyday Encounters*, Houndmills: Palgrave Macmillan, pp 15–42.

Office for National Statistics (ONS) (2011a) *Household Composition*. Census 2011. Available at: https://www.statistics.digitalresources.jisc.ac.uk/dataset/household-composition-persons-2011

Office for National Statistics (ONS) (2011b) *Neighbourhood Statistics*. Available at: https://www.ons.gov.uk/peoplepopulationandcommunity/populationandmigration/populationestimates/bulletins/2011censusquickstatisticsforenglandandwales/2013-01-30

Owen, M. (2009) *North Wales Male Voice Choirs*, Pwllheli: Llygad Gwalch.

Owen, T.M. (1956) 'The "communion season" and Presbyterianism in a Hebridean community', *Gwerin*, 1(2): 53–66.

Owen, T.M. (1986) 'Community studies in Wales', *Ethnologia Europaea*, XV: 27–52.

Pahl, R. (1965) 'Class and community in English commuter villages', *Sociologia Ruralis*, 5(1): 5–23.

Pahl, R. (1966) 'The rural-urban continuum', *Sociologia Ruralis*, 6(3): 299–329.

Pahl, R. (1968) *Readings in Urban Sociology*, Oxford: Pergamon Press.

Pahl, R. (1996) 'Friendly society', in S. Kraemer and J. Roberts (eds) *The Politics of Attachment*, London: Free Association Books, pp 88–101.

Pahl, R. (2005) 'Are all communities communities in the mind?', *The Sociological Review*, 53(4): 621–40.

Pahl, R. (2008) 'Hertfordshire commuter villages: from geography to sociology', *International Journal of Social Research Methodology*, 11(2): 103–7.

Pateman, C. (1988) 'The fraternal social contract', in J. Keane (ed) *Civil Society and the State: New European Perspectives*, London: Verso, pp 101–27.

Pearce, J. (2002) *Civil Society and Development: A Critical Exploration*, Boulder: Lynne Rienner Publishers.

Pérez-Díaz, V. (2014) 'Civil society: a multi-layered concept', *Current Sociology*, 62(6): 812–30.

Pestoff, V. (2006) 'Citizens and co-production of welfare services: childcare in eight European countries', *Public Management Review*, 8(4): 503–19.

Portmadoc-Jones, B. (1981) *Through These Windows, A Place and Its People,* Denbigh.

Purcell, M. (2006) 'Urban democracy and the local trap', *Urban Studies,* 43(11): 1921–41.

Pusey, M. (1998) 'Economic rationalism, human rights and civil society', *Australian Journal of Human Rights,* 4(2): 131–52.

Putnam, R. (2000) *Bowling Alone: The Collapse and Revival of American Community,* New York: Simon and Schuster.

Rapport, N. (1993) *Diverse World-Views in an English Village,* Edinburgh: Edinburgh University Press.

Rees, A.D. ([1950] 1975) *Life in a Welsh Countryside: A Social Study of Llanfihangel yng Ngwynfa,* Cardiff: University of Wales Press.

Richardson, L. (2008) *DIY Community Action: Neighbourhood Problems and Community Self-help,* Bristol: Policy Press.

Roberts, B. (1999) 'Time, biography and ethnic and national identity formation', in K.J. Brehony and N. Rassool (eds) *Nationalisms Old and New,* London: Palgrave Macmillan, pp 194–207.

Rogers, E. (1963) 'The history of trade unionism in the coal mining industry of North Wales to 1914', *Denbighshire Historical Society Transactions,* 12.

Rootes, C. (2008) *Acting Locally: Local Environmental Mobilizations and Campaigns,* London: Routledge.

Rose, N. (1996) 'The death of the social? Re-figuring the territory of government', *Economy and Society,* 25(3): 327–56.

Rosser, C. and Harris, C. (1965) *The Family and Social Change,* London: Routledge & Kegan Paul.

Routledge, P. (2003) 'Convergence space: process geographies of grassroots globalization networks', *Transactions of the Institute of British Geographers,* 28(3): 333–49.

Rucht, D. (2011) 'Civil society and civility in twentieth-century theorising', *European Review of History,* 18(3): 387–407.

Russell, C. (2021) 'Getting to authentic co-production: an asset-based community development perspective on co-production', in E. Loeffler and T. Bovaird (eds) *The Palgrave Handbook of Co-Production of Public Services and Outcomes,* New York: Springer International Publishing, pp 173–92.

Sassen, S. (2002) 'Global cities and diasporic networks: microsites in global civil society', in M. Glasius, M. Kaldor and H. Anheier (eds) *Global Civil Society Yearbook, 2002,* Oxford: Oxford University Press, pp 217–40.

Savage, M. (2008) 'Histories, belongings, communities', *International Journal of Social Research Methodology,* 11(2): 151–62.

Savage, M. (2010) 'The politics of elective belonging', *Housing, Theory and Society,* 27(2): 115–35.

Savage, M. and Warde, A. (1993) *Urban Sociology, Capitalism and Modernity,* London: Macmillan.

Savage, M., Bagnall, G. and Longhurst, B. (2005) *Globalization and Belonging*, London: Sage.

Savage, M., Li, Y. and Tampubolon, G. (2009) 'Rethinking the politics of social capital: challenging Tocquevillian perspectives', in R. Edwards, J. Franklin and J. Holland (eds) *Assessing Social Capital: Concept, Policy and Practice*, Cambridge: Cambridge Scholars Publishing, pp 70–94.

Schütze, F. and Schröder-Wildhagen, A. (2012) 'European mental space and its biographical relevance', in R. Miller, and G. Day (eds) *The Evolution of European Identities: Biographical Approaches*, London: Palgrave Macmillan, pp 255–78.

Seligman, A.B. (1992) *The Idea of Civil Society*, Princeton: Princeton University Press.

Seligman, A.B. (2000) *The Problem of Trust*, Princeton: Princeton University Press.

Sharpe, I. (2009) 'Empire, patriotism and the working class electorate: the 1900 General Election in the Battersea Constituency', *Parliamentary History*, 28(3): 392–412.

Short, B. (1992) 'The evolution of contrasting communities within rural England', in D.R. Mills (ed) *The English Rural Community*, London: Macmillan, pp 19–43.

Smith, D.H. (1983) 'Synanthrometrics: on the progress in the development of a general theory of voluntary action and citizen participation', in D.H. Smith and J. van Til (eds) *International Perspectives on Voluntary Action Research*, Washington, DC: University Press of America, pp 80–94.

Smith, D.H. (1994) 'Determinants of voluntary association participation and volunteering: a literature review', *Nonprofit and Voluntary Sector Quarterly*, 23(3): 243–63.

Somers, M.R. (1993) 'Citizenship and the place of the public sphere: law, community, and political culture in the transition to democracy', *American Sociological Review*, 58(5): 557–620.

Soteri-Proctor, A., Phillimore, J. and McCabe, A. (2013) 'Grassroots civil society at the crossroads: staying on the path to independence or turning onto the UK Government's route to localism?', *Development in Practice*, 23(8): 1022–33.

Stacey, M. (1960) *Tradition and Change: A Study of Banbury*, Oxford: Oxford University Press.

Strathern, M. (1981) *Kinship at the Core: An Anthropology of Elmdon, a Village in North West Essex in the Nineteen Sixties*, Cambridge: Cambridge University Press.

Tam, H. (1998) *Communitarianism: A New Agenda for Politics and Citizenship*, London: Macmillan.

Taylor, P.J. (2004) 'The new geography of global civil society: NGOs in the world city network', *Globalizations*, 1(2): 265–77.

Thompson-Fawcett, M. (2003) '"Urbanist" lived experience: resident observations on life in Poundbury', *Urban Design International*, 8(1): 67–84.

Tomaney, J. (2013) 'Parochialism: a defence', *Progress in Human Geography*, 37(5): 658–72.

Tönnies, F. ([1887] 2001) *Community and Civil Society*, J. Harris (ed), Cambridge: Cambridge University Press.

Uhlin, A. (2006) *Post-Soviet Civil Society: Democratization in Russia and the Baltic States*, London: Routledge.

Urry, J. (2000) 'Mobile sociology', *British Journal of Sociology*, 51(1): 185–203.

Wagner, P. (ed) (2006) *The Languages of Civil Society*, Oxford: Berghahn Books.

Wallman, S. (1984) *Eight London Households*, London: Tavistock.

Wallman, S. (1986) 'Ethnicity and the boundary process in context', in J. Rex and D. Mason (eds) *Theories of Race and Ethnic Relations*, Cambridge: Cambridge University Press, pp 226–45.

Walzer, M. (1992) 'The civil society argument', in C. Mouffe (ed) *Dimensions of Radical Democracy: Pluralism, Citizenship, Community*, London: Verso, pp 89–107.

Warde, A., Tampubolon, G., Longhurst, B., Ray, K., Savage, M. and Tomlinson, M. (2003) 'Trends in social capital: membership of associations in Great Britain 1991–98', *British Journal of Political Science*, 33: 515–25.

Wellman, B. (1979) 'The community question: the intimate networks of East Yorkers', *American Journal of Sociology*, 84(5): 1201–31.

Wellman, B. (ed) (1999) *Networks in the Global Village: Life in Contemporary Communities*, Boulder: Westview Press.

Welsh Government (2014) *Statistical Bulletin: National Survey for Wales, 2013–14, Volunteering and Caring*, Cardiff.

Welsh Government (2017) *National Survey for Wales, 2016–17: Volunteering and Caring*, Cardiff.

Welsh Joint Education Committee (WJEC) (2016) *Welsh Baccalaureate National Foundation Specification*, Cardiff: WJEC/WBAC. Available at: www.wjec.co.uk/qualifications/welsh-baccalaureate-national-foundation/#tab_overview

Wessendorf, S. (2014) '"Being open, but sometimes closed": conviviality in a super-diverse London neighbourhood', *European Journal of Cultural Studies*, 17(4): 392–405.

Wheeler, R. (2017) 'Local history as productive nostalgia? Change, continuity and sense of place in rural England', *Social and Cultural Geography*, 18(4): 466–86.

Williams, R. (1960) *Border Country*, London: Chatto and Windus.

Williams, R. (1973) *The City and the Country*, London: Chatto and Windus.

Williams, R. (1979) *The Fight For Manod*, London: Chatto and Windus.

Williams, R. (1983) *Resources of Hope*, London: Verso Press.

Williams, R. (1987) *The English Novel from Dickens to Lawrence*, London: Hogarth Press.

Williams, W. (1956) *The Sociology of an English Village: Gosforth*, London: Routledge.

Willmott, P. (1986) *Social Networks, Informal Care and Public Policy*, London: Policy Studies Institute.

Willmott, P. and Young, M. (1960) *Family and Class in a London Suburb*, London: Routledge.

Wilson, P. and Pahl, R. (1988) 'The changing sociological construct of the family', *The Sociological Review*, 36(2): 233–66.

Wirth, L. (1938) 'Urbanism as a way of life', *American Journal of Sociology*, 44(1): 1–24.

Young, I.M. (1986) 'The ideal of community and the politics of difference', *Social Theory and Practice*, 12(1): 1–26.

# Index

## A
Aberdaron 46
Aberporth 46
Aberystwyth 41
Abram, S. 32
Abrams, P. 34, 35–7
ACORN 56
action, local 33
action-orientated civil society 8
Adam, B. 32, 33, 71
Adult Learning 92
age 27, 67, 119
  age profiles 56–8, 103
ageing
  ageing congregations 92
  ageing members of the W.I. 97
  ageing volunteers 94
Agnew, J.A. 22
Alexander, J.C. 11, 14–15, 22
Alexander, J.-C. 12
Allan, G. 30, 33
Amin, A. 19, 21, 28
Amit, V. 42
Anderson, B. 15, 32
anthropological view 1, 42, 45, 47
anti-globalisation protests 13
Arato, A. 13
arts activities 94, 109
Ashmore, R.D. 72
asset-based development 127
associational life *see* associations
associations 1, 9, 16, 26, 82, 125
  associative practices 67
  and civil society 86–8, 100–2
  and conviviality 42
  decline in participation 26
  new forms of 26, 42–3
  in Overton 96–100
  in Rhos 53–4, 88–96
  and sustainability 100, 102
austerity 10, 29, 36, 87, 102

## B
Back, L. 21, 24–5
backward-looking 81, 84
Banbury 26
Band of Hope 67
Bangladeshi migrants 41–2
Barnardo's 87
Barrett, G. 22, 25, 81, 82
Battersea 38, 40
'Battle of Cinder Hill' 53
Baumgarten, B. 28

BBC 95
begging 108
'*beindin*' 75
Bell, C. 19, 21, 40
Bell, M.M. 44
belonging 3, 24, 30, 49, 72, 83, 126
  elective belonging 39, 40, 65, 99, 101
  and place 84
  sense of 111, 119
'below the radar' 2, 28, 29, 58, 65
Bennett, J. 75, 82
Benson, M. 21, 49, 65, 67
Berger, P.L. 73
Berman, S. 10
Best, E. 89
Bethnal Green 36, 41
Bhatt, M.G. 13
Big Society 1, 2, 10, 29, 102
'Big State' 13
biographies 125
  biographical attachments 123
  biographical methods 126
  biographical narratives 5–6, 72–3, 106–15
  and social structures 103
  *see also* case studies
Blokland, T. 75, 81
Blythe, R. 44
border country 48, 55
Born, B. 21–2
'bottom-up' initiatives 120, 127
boundaries 6, 24, 38, 45, 47, 69, 84
  boundary relationships 14
  between state and civil society 86
  symbolic boundaries 76, 81, 83
Bow 38, 41
bowling 88, 89–92, 95, 105
*Bowling Alone* 26
Boyle, P. 40
Brehm, J.M. 48
Bristol 18, 20
British National Party 41
Bruce, S. 92
Buchowski, M. 15
Bulmer, M. 34, 35, 37

## C
Cabinet Office 60
Calhoun, C. 16, 18–19
Cameron, David 29
Cameron, H. 27
campaigns 13, 18, 69, 96, 108
Cardiganshire 46
Caribbean-born people 38

car ownership 64
Carter, H. 32
case studies
　Cai's case 109–11
　Ifor from Rhos 71, 74–7, 81
　Karen's case 113–16
　Linda from Overton 71, 77–9
　Susan's case 111–13
　William's case 107–9
Castells, M. 13, 17
Census 2011 51, 58, 60
Chambers, S. 16
change 63, 113
　resistance to 115
chapel 46, 53, 54, 88, 92, 107
　and family 93
　youth groups 67
charitable patterns 118
Charles, N. 41–2
Cheadle 40
childcare 113–14, 122
childhood 104
children 56, 76, 89, 91, 105, 122
choirs 53, 54, 65, 101, 117
Christianity, ' alternative' 92
church, Anglican parish 4, 55, 79, 92, 98–9
Church, Methodist 98
church services 88, 98
cities 11, 19, 20
　and social differentiation 49
citizen involvement 117
citizenship 9, 97, 126
civil disobedience 72
civility 2, 9, 26, 43, 103, 125, 126
　and rural communities 31–2
civil rights 13
civil society 1–4, 16, 18–19, 83–4
　and associations 43, 86–8, 100–2
　and community 24–6
　defining 8–14, 126
　and economic change 115–18
　and the economy and state 103
　as a field of action 9–10, 15
　global 17–19
　and government policy 127
　and the life cycle 104–5
　narratives of 71–4, 80, 83
　participation in 4, 125
　progressive 18–19, 38, 41, 127
　state relationship with 14
　and the village 45–50, 65–9
class 11, 45, 48, 65, 87, 101, 103
　identity and culture 26–7
　and place 106
　see also middle-class, working-class
Cloke, P. 44
closure 25, 32, 43, 47, 127
Cnaan, R.A. 105

coal seam 52
'Cocoa and Reading Rooms' 55
Coflein 55
Cohen, A. 13, 30, 46, 48
Cohen, J.L. 15
Cohen, P. 24
collective action 12, 37, 115
collective participation 99
commitment 10, 19, 28, 34, 81, 95, 104, 117
common good 10
common interests 1, 3, 9, 86, 97
communism 12
Communities First 92
community 4, 8, 28, 33, 34, 96
　and associations 87, 126
　charity 118–19
　and civil society 24–6
　Community Chest Fund 90, 101
　councillor 99–100, 112, 114, 123
　'knowable community' 48
　nature of 19–22, 26–34, 30–4, 73
　newspapers 93–4
　studies 24, 34, 35, 126–7
*Community and Civil Society* 11
Community Café 89–92, 95
Community Life Survey 60
commuting 36
conflict and division 47, 50, 86
Conservative-Liberal Government 10, 29
consultation 113, 116, 123
contextual factors and the villages 51–2
continuities/discontinuities 26, 34, 38–42, 80, 83, 126
conviviality 3, 24, 31, 42–3, 126, 127
cooperation 2, 13, 82, 126
Cornwall, A. 50
cosmopolitanism 18–19, 24
council employees 91
COVID-19 2
Crehan, K. 14, 33
Cresswell, T. 31, 72
crime 63
cross-border connections 5
cross-generational interaction 95
Crow, G. 30
crowd-funding 118, 119, 123
Crown Green bowling 89, 90
culture 4, 50, 61, 63, 65
　cultural exchange 97
　cultural heritage of Rhos 109–10
　cultural life 117
　erosion of Welsh culture 92

**D**

Dallimore, D.J. 2, 59, 102
dance groups 96
da Silva, D.S. 117
Davies, C.A. 41–2

Davies, E. 46
Davies, J. 52
Davis, H. 88, 92
Dawson, M.T.C. 13
Day, G. 25, 30, 45, 48, 81
*De Cive* 11
democracy 9, 12, 17, 117
Dench, G. 41
Dennis, N. 107
deprivation 28, 29, 58, 97
deregulation 28, 29
devolution 5, 51
dialect 61, 76, 81
Diani, M. 18
differences, recognition of 24, 126
disadvantaged communities 28
diversity 20, 25
division and conflict 47, 50, 86
Dodd, A.H. 52
donations *see* funding
Done, B. 55
drama 53, 66, 67, 109–10
Dunn, E. 13
Durkheim, E. 11, 36

# E

East End 38, 41
Eastern Europe 12, 13
economic change 115–19
economic relations 103
economic solidarities 123
editorial board 76, 77
Edmondson, R. 33
education 77
Edward I 55
Edwards, M. 87
Eisteddfod 65, 89
elected representatives 91
elective belonging 24, 39, 40, 65, 82, 99, 101
Elias, N. 30, 40
Ellis, K. 94
Elmdon 40
embodied attachments 103
Emmett, I. 49
emotional local ties 72, 73, 83, 84
  *see also* elective belonging
employment 4, 28, 35, 46, 75, 104
  as a miner 107
  opportunities for 109, 115, 121
  professionals 106
  types of 57–8
  women in 117
  worsening conditions 27
  *see also* unemployment
empowerment 116
England 5, 26, 48
  English villages 44, 45
entertainment personality 110

entrepreneurship 116–18, 122
environmental issues 105, 122
equality/inequality 2, 27, 28, 43, 87, 101
*Essay on the History of Civil Society* 10
estate system 56, 78
ethical teachings 53
ethnicity 38, 41
  BAME 18, 38
  Black and Caribbean-born people 38
  ethnic chauvinism 51
  ethnic homogeneity 45
  ethnic identities 32
  White people 6, 27, 41, 42
Etzioni, A. 28
Evers, A. 30
everyday living 17, 24, 42–3, 72
  spheres of life 47
exclusion 63, 76–7, 80, 81, 127

# F

Facebook 69, 98
facilities, poor 61, 64
Falk, R. 9
family 16, 46, 68, 100, 104, 107
  and chapel 93
  and Welsh language 63
Fascism 20
female work, unpaid 10
feminist critiques 10
Ferguson, A. 10, 11, 20
Flaherty, M.G. 32
Flintshire 55
food banks 119
forward-looking 82, 84
Frakenberg, R. 44, 46, 47, 50, 53, 64
French twinning association 96–7
funding 5, 83, 87, 101–2, 120
  of associations 86
  charitable patterns 118
  of the Community Café 92
  Community Chest Fund 90
  fundraising events 97
  grant funding 89, 91, 93–4
  place-based 126, 127
  of the Ponciau Park 91
  of the Stiwt 94
Fyfe, N. 28, 29

# G

Gans, H.J. 21, 34
gender 119
  gendered economic relations 103, 105
  gender relations 113
generational divide 105
Georgiou, M. 2, 43
Giddens 28
Gilroy, P. 25
Glan-llyn 46
Glasgow 18, 28

global civil society 17
globalisation 13, 17, 39
Gluckman, Max 47
Glynceiriog 46, 49, 50
Glyndwr, Owain 55
good life 103, 123
good society 8, 14, 119
Gøtzsche-Astrup, J. 14
Government of Wales Act 1988 5
government policy 6, 28–9, 123
  Big Society 1, 2, 10, 29, 102
  Labour's Third Way 21, 28
  'light-touch' support 127
  local policy alignment 121–3
  privatisation 13
  *see also* miner's strike (1984-5)
graduates 97
Gramsci, A. 11–12, 14
grant funding 87, 91, 93–4
grassroots action 1, 14, 18, 119, 121
Greater Manchester 39
Green Flag Award 90
'Greenleigh' 40
Grenier, P. 27, 87
Guma, T. 41
Gustafson, P. 48

## H

Habermas, J. 17
Halfacree, K. 40
Hall, P.A. 27
Halpern, D. 27
Hambleton, R. 2, 3
Han, J. 13
Hancock, L. 28
Hann, C. 13
hard work 75
Harper, S. 44
Harvey, D. 20–1
Hayek 28
healthy living issues 105
Hebridean communities 46
Hegel 11
Heley, J. 22
heritage 33, 88, 120
  funding 84
  heritage based community 31
  heritage role 96, 109, 121, 125
heterogeneous communities 37–8
Hirst, P. 117
history 50, 69
  local 33
  of the villages 52–6
Hobbes, T. 10, 11, 20
Hobsbawm, E.J. 20
Hoggett, P. 28
homogenous communities 37–8, 49
housing 38, 39, 55
  poor 127

housing development 69, 78, 101, 106, 111–13
Huddersfield 26
Hughes, G. 93, 94
Hyde, C. 16, 30

## I

identity 12, 25, 60, 64, 69
  shared identities 47
  strong identities 101
immigrants 38
improving the locality 125
incivility 24
inclusion 3, 41, 45, 82
income, household 57, 107
incomers 5, 38, 43, 92, 96, 98, 101, 102, 126
  elective belonging 39–40, 82–3
  migration to villages 49, 78
  negative views of 63
  *see also* outsiders
indigenous communities 43
individuals 103, 116
  and associations 27
  empowering 29
  individual biographies 71, 125
  key 4, 29
  and spirituality 93
industrial action 108
industrial decline 72
industrialisation 52
industrial past 40, 46, 54, 65, 88, 100
inequality *see* equality/inequality
informal networks 13, 36
Ingen, R.R.W. 53
insecurity 35
insider/outsider dynamics 2, 40
institutions 119, 120, 121, 122, 123, 127
international experience 126
international institutions 13
International Monetary Fund 13
international volunteering 89, 101
Ireland 33
Irish Sea 51
isolation 32, 35, 47, 48
isomorphism 17, 47

## J

Jackson, A.J.H. 56
Jackson, B. 26, 90
Jackson, E. 21
Jenkins, D. 46
Jessop, B. 80, 81, 83
job security 107
Jones, Emrys 46
Jones, L. 22, 104
Jones-Hughes, T. 46

## K

Kaldor, M. 8, 10, 13, 14, 17, 18, 71

Keane, J. 11–12
Keep Wales Tidy 99, 112
Kisby, B. 29
Kitchen, L. 48

**L**

labour
  market flexibility 28
  movement 23
  worsening conditions 27
Labour's Third Way 21, 28
Laidlaw, R. 52, 53, 54, 58, 67
Lancee, B. 104, 105
Latin America 12
leadership 96, 122–3
legacy 125
Leland, John 55
Levitas, R. 1, 28
Lewicka, M. 48, 60
Lewis, D. 13
Lewis, G.J. 46
Lewis, J. 86
Liberal Democrats 41
libraries 6, 28, 59, 119
Liepins, R. 25
life cycle 99, 104–5
*Life in a Welsh Countryside* 45
lifelong commitment 4, 9, 77, 81–2
lifelong connections 3
life stories *see* biographies
lifestyles 44
Linda from Overton 71, 77–9
litter-picking 66, 99, 112, 121
Littlejohn, J. 44
Llanfihangel 44–5
Llanfrothen 49
Lloyd George, Megan 89
Llyn peninsula 46
local and global 18–19, 24, 25
local associational life 86–8
  *see also* associations
local authorities 91, 94, 95, 119
  funding 87
local economy 103, 116–18, 122
local leadership 122–3
local protest 18, 29
  *see also* housing developments
Locke, J. 10
Lofland, L.H. 42
London 20, 36, 38, 40, 41
long-term residents 40
Low, S.M. 48
lunch clubs 68
Lynch, K. 73

**M**

*Maelor* 51–2
male voice choirs 54, 101, 105
Manchester 39, 40

Mann, R. 40
marital and partnership status 56
marketisation of the third sector 86
market liberalisation 29
Marshall, T.F. 29
Marx, K. 12
Massey, D. 19, 21, 24, 31
McBeath, G. 20
McCabe, A. 2, 28, 29, 65, 86
McCulloch, A. 27, 28
McFarlane, C. 18
McIlwaine, C. 18
Mead, G.H. 32
media 121
meeting places 29, 88, 91, 96
men 27, 42, 68, 105
  bowls club 90–2, 95
  and mining 107–8
methodology 4–6
Meyer, M. 16, 30
middle-class 26, 59, 78, 106
  membership of organisations 27
  migration to villages 40, 49, 56, 67
migration 18, 31, 45, 48, 60
  and industrialisation 52
  international 6
  migration to villages 49, 56, 67
  patterns 5
  refugees 40–1
Milbourne, P. 48
Milligan, C. 29
Mills, D.R. 56
Milltown 40
mining 35, 52–3, 75, 81, 88, 100
  decline of 54, 94, 115
  Miner's Institute 54, 89
  miners strike (1926) 89
  miners strike (1984-5) 107–9, 116
  mining heritage of Rhos 105–9
  *see also* Stiwt, the
mobility 36, 40, 45, 48
modern life 11, 36, 44
  modern neighbourhoodism 36, 37
Mohan, G. 28
Mooney, G. 28
Moore, R. 41
morals 75, 82
  moral ownership 40, 49, 64
Mosques 42
motherhood 105
  motherhood in Overton 113–15
multicultural places 25, 82
Murdoch, J. 25
music 4, 54, 63, 65, 96, 110
Muske, G. 119
mutual aid 37

**N**

narratives of time and place 71–4, 80–4

National Childminders Association 114
nationalisation 120
nationalism 16
National Lottery 87, 101, 114
  Heritage Lottery Fund (HLF) 89, 91, 94
National Survey of Wales 60, 63
Neal, S. 4, 32, 40, 42
neighbourhoods 2, 34, 35–7
*Nene* newspaper 52, 93–4
  funding 74–5
neo-liberalism 13, 28
networks 105, 106, 117
Newby, H. 19, 21, 44
newcomers 31, 37, 38, 43, 49, 76, 79, 82
New Deal for Communities 29
new housing developments *see* housing development
newspapers 52, 73, 74, 79, 88
  funding 74–5, 78
  *Nene* newspaper 93–4
  *Overton Oracle* 77–8, 83, 96, 99
NGOs 13, 14, 87
NIMBY 29
nonconformism 53, 56, 63, 88
non-profit enterprise 92
Norfolk 33
norms of civility 104, 119
North East Wales 4, 44, 54
nostalgia 32, 54, 95, 100, 126
  nostalgic narratives 71, 75, 80–4, 99
Nowicka, M. 42
NSPCC 87

## O

occupations *see* employment
Office for National Statistics (ONS) 51, 56, 60
older generations 56, 92, 97, 100, 105
online 78, 83, 117
  networks 36
open-cast pits 52
open/closed settlements 56
openness, tradition of 38
opposition to development *see* housing development
organisational structure 83
outsiders 2, 30, 31, 40, 63, 76, 92, 99
  *see also* incomers
Overton 4, 51, 55–6, 78–9, 82–3
  associations 66–7
*Overton Oracle* 66, 74, 77–8, 79, 83, 99
Owen, M. 101
Owen, T.-M. 45, 46, 47
owner-occupiers 58

## P

Pahl, R. 21, 30, 34, 40, 42, 49, 65, 67, 78
*Papurau Bro* 74, 93–4
parent and toddler group 66

parks *see* Ponciau Banks Park
parochialism 19, 29
participation 16, 50, 53, 68, 82, 87
  and biography 71–3
  in church events 99
  in civil society 125
  decline of 13
  female-driven 110
  nature of 27
  patterns of 87, 101, 103–4, 119, 123
  *see also* associations
past, preserving the 81
past and future, relationship between 33
Pateman, C. 10
patterns of association 100, 102
patterns of settlement 19
Pearce, J. 13
Peel, Robert and Anne 55
'Pentre' 47
Pérez-Díaz, V. 11
personal commitment 81–2, 95
Pestoff, V. 117
Phillimore, J. 28, 29
physical wealth 106
picket lines 108
place 21, 25, 30–3, 71, 106, 126
  and associations 88
  attachments to 3, 39, 48–9, 125
  narratives of 43
  and people 22
  place-identity 60–1
  rural urban distinctions 19–23
  symbolic landscape of 73
playgroups 77, 105
policy, government *see* government policy
policy alignment 121–3
policy protectionism 120–2
political activism 18
political landscapes 119, 122
political relations 103
Ponciau Banks Park 89–90, 101
poor communities 28, 29
poor families 97
Portmadoc-Jones, B. 53
post-industrial 101
post-war society 28, 36, 41, 120
post-war studies of rural Wales 46
power relations 14, 73, 123, 127
preserving the past 81
primary school 99
Prince of Wales 55
privatisation 13
professionals 27, 37, 101, 106
property prices 106
protecting the locality 125
'protective bubbles' 120, 121, 127
protests 28, 53, 108, 113, 116
public sphere, the 15–16, 17
pubs 53, 63, 64, 119

# Index

Purcell, M. 21
Pusey, M. 16
Putnam, R. 9, 13, 26, 27, 28, 87, 96

## Q
qualified population 101

## R
racism 41, 51, 127
Ramsbottom 40
Rapport, N. 44
recreational associations *see* associations
rector, the 98
Red Cross 87
Rees, A.D. 21, 32, 37, 45–6, 47
refugee crisis 41
regeneration programmes 29, 127
religion 4, 46, 56, 88, 95, 99
  declining religious attendance 92
  in Rhos 53
Remembrance rituals 99
retired people 58, 90, 97, 104
Rhos 4, 51, 52, 88, 89
  associations 65
  Christmas Panto 109–11, 117, 121
  history of 52–4
*Rhos Herald* 52, 54
Richardson, L. 28
Roberts, B. 33
Rogers, E. 53
rolling back the state 13, 29
Rootes, C. 18
Rose, N. 30
Rosser, C. 40
Routledge, P. 18
Rucht, D. 9, 28, 29–30, 43
rural community studies 45
rural idyll 4, 39, 44, 56, 65, 67
rural urban distinctions 11, 19–23, 32, 67, 101
Russell, C. 120

## S
Sassen, S. 18
Savage, M. 11, 27, 40, 64, 103, 106
  elective belonging 24, 38–40, 49, 65, 82, 99
schools 77
Schütze, F. 80
Scotson, J. 40
secularisation 59, 92, 93
self-government 84
self-images of the villages 59–65
Seligman, A.B. 10, 11–12
*Senedd see* Welsh Government
services, loss of 113
shared enterprises 3
shared spaces 'hubs' *see* meeting places
Sharpe, I. 38

Short, B. 56, 106
Silver Band 65
situated process 39
situational data 50
size of the community 50
skills 104, 106
slate quarries 46
Smith, D.H. 104
sociability 9, 28
social action 86, 110
social and economic factors 27, 50, 70
social change 26–30, 47
social class *see* class
social constraints 35
social media 95, 96
social movements 13, 14, 16, 18
social networks 31, 86
social relations 1, 2, 19, 45, 46, 48
socio-economic profiles of the villages 56–9
socio-spatial contexts 125
solidarity 3, 10, 31, 86, 108, 125
  and associations 102
  and civil society 15–16
  and collective action 28
  and donations 94
  economic solidarities 118–19, 123
  informal 98
  narratives of 80–1
  norms of 103
  political 48
Somers, M.R. 12
Soteri-Proctor, A. 28, 29
South London 38
Soviet Union 12
spheres of life 47
sponsorships 118, 123
sports organisations 4, 27, 53, 65, 66, 96, 105
  *see also* associations
SPSS software 60
'Squire, The' 78, 82
Stacey, M. 26, 40
state dependency 127
state institutions 103, 111, 119, 120
Stiwt, the 65, 75, 84, 89, 118, 121
  campaign to save 54, 69
  the clock 95
strangers 2, 24, 29, 63
  *see also* incomers, outsiders
Strathern, M. 40
stratification and participation 103–4
street survey 6, 59
strikes/pit closures *see* mining
subscriptions 94
succession 77, 98, 126
Sure Start 29
sustainability 125
Swansea 40, 41, 42
symbolic landscape 78

## T

Takeda, N. 30
Tam, H. 20
Taylor, P.J. 13
temperance 53, 55
theatre 65, 66
third sector 87
threats
  to places 33
  to services 37
  to way of life 116
time 3, 25, 26–34, 34, 71
  free time 104
  importance of 125
  representations of 32–3
Tocqueville 11–12, 26
Tomaney, J. 19, 33
Tönnies, F. 11, 19
top-down initiatives 29, 120
Tower Hamlets 41
trade unions 23, 26, 88, 107
traditional neighbourhoods 35, 36, 41
transfer of state functions 28
transnational civil society 17, 18
transport 36, 64
  Buses 64
Tregaron 46
trust 126
twinning association 66, 96–7

## U

Uhlin, A. 9
unemployment 35, 127
United Kingdom 2
urban village 21
Urry, J. 48

## V

values 1, 80, 125
*Village on the Border* 46
villages 11, 20, 45–51
  and the middle class 49
  village life 44, 84, 98–9
villages, the (Rhos and Overton) 4–5, 50–1
  associations 65–7
  civil society structures 65–9
  contextual factors 51–2
  history 52–6
  self-image 59–65
  socio-economic profiles 56–9
voluntary action 1, 2, 86, 87, 98, 122, 125
  and the Big Society 29, 102
  and economic factors 28
  international volunteering 89, 101
  levels of 50, 68
  and newspapers 93–4, 96
  and women 97–8

## W

Wagner, P. 10
Wales 5, 41, 45, 60, 63, 81
  Arts Council of Wales 94
  first female MP 89
  Keep Wales Tidy 99
  National Survey 60
  Welsh Baccalaureate 104
  Welsh Government 5, 51, 58, 60, 68, 93
  Welsh Index of Deprivation (WIMD) 58
  Welsh Joint Education Committee (WJEC) 104
  WISERD 4
  *see also* Welsh language, mining
walking groups 66
Wallman, S. 34, 37–8, 40, 41, 81
Warde, A. 11, 27
way of life 21, 41, 80, 107–8, 115, 116
wealth of communities 101, 118
Webb, S. 20
welfare state 28, 36, 117
Wellman, B. 32, 36–7
Welsh language 5, 51, 52, 58, 60, 95
  community newspaper 93–4
  erosion of 92
  and identity 63, 88
  media and arts 110–11
  in Overton 64
  Rhos dialect 74–7, 81
Welsh Language Board 121
*Welsh Rural Communities* 46
Wessendorf, S. 25, 31, 42
Western societies, decline in participation 13, 26, 87
Wheeler, R. 33
Williams, R. 22, 35, 48
Williams, W. 44
William's case 107–9
Wilmott, P. 36, 40, 41
Wilmslow 40
Wilson, P. 34
Wirth, P. 20
WISERD 4
women 10, 26, 41, 68, 90, 92, 117
Women's Institute 66, 96, 97–8, 105, 114
working-class 59, 101, 104, 106
  associations 26, 27, 53, 54, 97
  bowls club 90, 95
  culture 63, 65, 75, 88
  and democracy 12
  gentrification 39, 40
  heritage 81, 105
  work ethic 107
World Bank 13
Wrexham 86, 111
  Wrexham Borough Council 51, 89, 94, 95, 101, 102

Wright, K. 27, 87

**Y**

*Y Cymo* 93–4
yoga 66
Young, I.M. 20, 50

Young, M. 40
younger generations 56, 88, 92, 96, 98, 105, 114

**Z**

Zumba classes 105

www.ingramcontent.com/pod-product-compliance
Lightning Source LLC
Chambersburg PA
CBHW071713020426
42333CB00017B/2248